D0838588

AWAKENING TO THE LOTUS
an Introduction to Nichiren Shu

AWAKENING
TO THE
LOTUS
an Introduction to Nichiren Shu

Nichiren Buddhist International Center • Hayward, California

Nichiren Buddhist International Center
29490 Mission Boulevard
Hayward, California 94544

First Edition

10 9 8 7 6 5 4 3 2 1

ISBN: 0-9719645-0-5

Table *of* Contents

Preface

Although the Nichiren Shu school of Buddhism has 750 years of history in Japan and has been in the United States since 1900, this Buddhist organization is not yet well-known outside of Japan. When Nichiren Buddhism has been heard of at all, it is often confused with other groups who also chant "Namu Myoho Renge Kyo" and who claim Nichiren Shōnin as their founder. In an attempt to end this confusion and present the real Nichiren Shu, we are pleased to bring you this book, *Awakening to the Lotus*, to make the teachings and doctrine of our school clear.

This book was originally inspired by Dr. Hōyō Watanabe's book *Watashitachi no Nichiren Shu ("Our Nichiren Shu")*. Though the current book has been extensively adapted from Dr. Watanabe's text for Western readers, we are deeply indebted to his original work not only for the basic idea of the book, but also for some of this book's contents which were adapted from a translation of his book done by the Nichiren-shu Overseas Propagation Promotion Association.

By providing information about Nichiren Shu in this book, we hope to lead more people to the teachings of Sakyamuni Buddha and the teachings of Nichiren Shonin. In doing so, we hope to make their lives happier and the world a more peaceful place.

I would like to extend my most sincere thanks to the following individuals, without whom this project would not have been possible: Dr. Hōyō Watanabe, Nichiren Shu Shūmuin Headquarters, the Nichiren-shu Overseas Propagation Promotion Association, the Nichiren Shu Newspaper Company, Rev. Daniel Montgomery, Rev. Ryuoh Faulconer, John Petry, and Matt L. Miller.

Sincerely,
Rev. Ryuken Akahoshi
General Manager
Nichiren Buddhist International Center

March 31, 2003

Chapter 1
Nichiren Shu

The Nichiren Shu is a school of Buddhism—lay people, ministers, temples, and doctrines—that was founded in thirteenth century Japan by a Buddhist priest named Nichiren Shōnin. In Japan, Nichiren Shōnin is a well-known historical figure renowned for his steadfast determination in the face of religious persecution. In the same way, the Japanese people know the Nichiren Shu as a large religious institution with a long history of similar determination. In Western countries, however, most people have very little knowledge of Buddhism, much less any understanding of the various schools of thought that have come into being during Buddhism's 2500 year history.

Nichiren Shōnin himself did not originally intend to found a new school of Buddhism. In fact, he said in one of his many writings, "I am neither the founder of any school nor the inheritor of any lineage." However, it was his intention to reform Buddhism, which had become weighted down with scholarly theories and esoteric rituals. Ordinary people could not understand Buddhist teachings, and only the very wealthy could afford to fund the performance of intricate and lavish mystical ceremonies that many schools required. Further, there were some  schools of Buddhism that entirely corrupted the Buddha's teachings with oversimplifications; those schools were probably reactions to the first two problems.

Nichiren Shōnin wanted to find the true teaching of the Buddha and make the Buddha's teaching once again accessible to all people. Like many of the people of his age, he wished to relieve the widespread suffering of medieval society. He found his answers in the *Lotus Sutra*. As he understood the Buddha's teachings more deeply and lived the words of the sutra in his own life, he was able to extract the essence of

Buddhism from within the sutra and develop a Buddhist practice and theory that was accessible to all people.

In this book, we will look at the school that Nichiren Shōnin founded and the roots of its beliefs. First, we will briefly examine the basic doctrines of Nichiren Shu and of general Buddhism. Next, we will take a look at the life of Nichiren Shōnin: his search for the Buddha's highest teaching and his journey in revealing those teachings. Then we will take a look at the teachings themselves: Nichiren Shōnin's writings and the *Lotus Sutra*. Finally, we will examine putting those teachings and doctrines into practice. The final portion is, therefore, the most important—in Buddhism, practice is as important as doctrine. Practice is the foundation for understanding the doctrines, so it may be considered even more important in some ways. Practice is often best learned and perfected with help from current practitioners.

Because this book is only an introduction to Nichiren Shu, there will often be more detailed information available. The bibliography lists resources for more detailed study of doctrine, Nichiren Shōnin's life, the *Lotus Sutra*, and the basics of practice.

Chapter 2
Doctrine

Tradition says that the Buddha taught over eighty thousand sutras during his life, so it would be very difficult to learn all of the Buddha's teachings. Fortunately, it is not necessary to study all of the sutras to understand Buddhism.

There are key teachings, derived from the eighty thousand or more sutras, that all Buddhists regard as the basis of Buddhist doctrine. In discussing the doctrines of Nichiren Shu, we will start with these basic teachings. We will then move on to teachings that are more specific to Nichiren Buddhism. This discussion will only lightly touch on these basic doctrines; for a deeper understanding of Buddhist doctrine, more study would be useful. It will be helpful to remember that many of the Buddha's teachings cover the same idea from different perspectives. The Buddha taught using many different methods so that all his followers could understand and grow toward the goal of enlightenment. When dealing with subtle truths such as the nature of reality, different people require different ways of teaching to understand the same concepts. This is why the Buddha's teachings sometimes appear to be different on the surface, but contain similarities and common threads that tie them all together.

Basic Buddhist Doctrines

When the Buddha first reached supreme enlightenment, he discovered the true nature of all things in the universe and the laws that govern all aspects of life. Of course, this discovery was extremely complicated; if he attempted to teach it to people in its entirety from the beginning, they would never be able to understand it. It would be like trying to teach a child who does not know simple math how to do calculus. Therefore, the Buddha broke his teaching into progressively more profound parts so that he could bring people to understanding.

The Four Noble Truths

The first thing the Buddha taught was the Four Noble Truths. Put simply, these are:

Life is Suffering.
There is a cause for Suffering.
Suffering can be overcome.
The way to overcome suffering is the Eightfold Path.

What did the Buddha mean by saying, "Life is Suffering"? When we look at it more closely, this is not a depressing statement as it might seem to be. What is the most important thing that we, as humans, are

looking for? Our goal is happiness, but even when we achieve happiness it never seems to last. The Buddha saw that we are struggling in this life trying to survive and to be happy. Many obstacles appear that stop us from getting happiness or from keeping it. When we are young, we do not always get what we want. As we get older, this is reemphasized as we discover that we need money to buy the things that we think we need. Relationships also can be very happy times until they disintegrate. Some couples tire of each other and break up. Others lose their loved ones to sickness and death. Some of us do not like our jobs and feel trapped in them. Others love their jobs but end up working with one person who always gets on their nerves. There is always something that keeps us from perfect

The Buddha teaching for the first time after his enlightenment.

happiness. The car needs repairs, the bills are late, the in-laws are nagging—the list could be endless. The unsatisfactory nature of life is summarized in Buddhism by the "Four Sufferings," which are birth (called suffering because it inevitably leads to the next three), old age, sickness, and death. A more complete explanation of suffering—and a further expansion on why birth is considered suffering—is found in the "Eight Sufferings." These eight include the Four Sufferings and adds the suffering of beings separated from loved ones and other things one desires to keep, encountering people or circumstances that one dislikes, not being able to get things that one desires, and being attached to things that are impermanent, including one's own mind and body.

This leads us to the second Noble Truth, which can be summarized as "cause and effect." You may have heard of karma and wondered what it is. Simply put, it is cause and effect. Many common ideas and old sayings reflect the idea of karma, such as, "what goes around comes around" and "one who lives by the sword dies by the sword". These old phrases have already started us down the path of learning about cause and effect. For every action that we make, a reaction occurs. For example, if you put hot water in a cup and add a tea bag soon you will have tea. If you leave it in too long, it may be bitter; if you do not leave it in long enough, it may be weak. Obviously, understanding karma is more complex than understanding the brewing of tea, but this example is the start in understanding the big picture of how cause and effect works. Many factors may be involved in the cause and they all will affect the result. Suffering itself also has a cause. Because we can look at the causes of suffering, we can start to understand suffering and eliminate it or at least lessen it.

That brings us to the third Noble Truth: Suffering can be overcome. We cannot make all the bad things that happen in our lives go away, but we can understand them more deeply and learn from them. We soon will understand that suffering is optional. It helps to make a distinction between pain and suffering. Pain is the feeling we experience in our bodies when something happens that we do not like. Suffering is how we handle the pain in our minds. Pain does not necessarily lead to suffering. Many people will tolerate pain if they know that through it some greater good will come. Athletes in particular are notorious for "playing through pain" in order to gain a victory. The Buddha taught that we can reduce the amount of suffering in our lives.

The Eightfold Path

This leads to the Fourth Noble Truth: how to stop this cycle of suffering, worrying, and being depressed. The Buddha tells us it is as simple as following the Eightfold Path. The Eightfold Path is a set of guidelines for our lives that help us develop understanding and compassion. Developing that kind of deeply compassionate life can help release us from suffering. The Eightfold Path is:

Right Views,
Right Thought,
Right Speech,
Right Action,
Right Livelihood,

Right Effort,
Right Mindfulness, and
Right Meditation

Some people are confused by the use of the word "right" in the Eightfold Path. Words such as appropriate, thoughtful, or correct could also be used to explain these eight dimensions of the Buddha's path. Since most scholars use "right" when translating the steps of the Eightfold Path, we will continue to use that word here. So what exactly do we mean by "right"? It means that we should use our judgment based on the Buddha's teachings and be mindful of these things when living with others in our society. When looking at a situation, we should get all the information so we can have right views. Without all the information we may make an incorrect assumption. We should try not to think of things which could harm others if we were to actually do what we thought about. We should think about what we say. Is what we are saying going to hurt someone or will it benefit them? Is our job productive and helpful to our fellow beings, or are we doing something dishonest or destructive to our neighbors or the planet? When we eat, do we consider everything that went into that meal? The sun, moon, the soil, the rain, the farmer planting the seed and harvesting the crops, the wholesaler, the market and the people who work there, the cook who prepared the meal—all of these make our meal possible. We should always be mindful and remember that things do not just appear out of thin air for our benefit. We can increase the mindfulness in our views, thought, speech, actions, livelihood, and effort by practicing meditation. It is through our practice of the Eightfold Path that we move towards enlightenment.

Mahāyāna Buddhism

After the Buddha passed away, his followers tried to keep all of his teachings in order. Because of the hardships of communication and travel, different schools of thought arose out of the Buddhist tradition. Theravada (a Pali word meaning the "way of the elders") Buddhism spread mostly in Southeast Asia. Mahāyāna (the "great vehicle" in Sanskrit) Buddhism spread north into China, Korea, and Japan.

Theravadan Buddhism focuses on practicing as a monk or nun. Some people would become monks or nuns and live very simple lives in a monastery. It was generally accepted that it would take many lifetimes to become enlightened like the Buddha. Lay people were not considered to be following the path to enlightenment and only received benefit by supporting the monastic practitioners.

Mahāyāna Buddhism developed over the first few centuries after the Buddha died. This form of Buddhism taught the bodhisattva way. A bodhisattva is someone who has reached a high state of realization and can enter into nirvana, but decides to stay in this world to help others reach the goal of enlightenment before he or she takes that final step. The wonderful ideal of this school of Buddhism is that all of us, both clergy and lay people, can some day reach enlightenment. A bodhisattva practices the Six Perfections or *pāramitās* to obtain the goal of causing all beings to strive for Buddhahood.

The Six Perfections are:

Giving
Observing Precepts
Patience
Striving
Meditation
Wisdom

When looking at these, you may see similarities to the Eightfold Path. The Six Perfections reflect the basic values of the Eightfold Path, but give them a different focus.

Giving is something we should do from our hearts. Giving in the Six Perfections does not necessarily refer to giving money. It can be giving a lesson, giving time, or giving an ear to listen. In other words, this giving is sharing our resources—time, learning, emotional support, or money—to help others. It is important that this giving be done without regret and not grudgingly. Giving should never be done simply out of a sense of duty, but rather out of compassion.

The precepts that the Six Perfections ask us to keep are guidelines for behavior that we should constantly keep in mind. The precepts followed by Mahāyāna Buddhists are:

Not to kill
Not to steal
Not to indulge in harmful sexual behavior
Not to lie
Not to take intoxicants

The precepts should be observed in the spirit of "the Golden Rule." We should do to others as we would have others do to us. The heart of the precepts is the desire to avoid hurting others and to prevent our actions from causing suffering for our fellow beings.

Patience can be one of the most difficult virtues for many people today to practice. We live in a very busy world where time is measured and treasured. Patience is necessary for us to practice compassion and mindfulness. Are we really in such a hurry? Often, when we rush ourselves and others, we lose the meaning and joy in the time that we struggle so hard to save.

Striving means to keep moving forward. Sometimes things get rough, like when you go on a diet. Even though you hit a plateau and stop losing weight, you need to persevere. Soon the weight will start going down again. Likewise, our Buddhist practice is difficult; sometimes we get emotional. It is difficult to be nice to the customer who is yelling at you or the person who cuts you off in traffic. However, through striving to maintain our practice, the Six Perfections get easier to maintain. Meditation focuses our mind and allows us to be mindful, patient, and giving.

Wisdom soon develops out of our practice. As you learn these concepts you will realize that all the practices of the Six Perfections are tied together. For example, when teaching people something new, we sometimes need patience while they slowly learn the concepts that we are instructing them in. Sometimes we need to persevere when they do not get a concept right away and perhaps try another approach that is easier for them. There are many examples of how the Six Perfections can be applied in your daily life, but it is important to remember that they must not only be learned but they must also be practiced to have an impact on your life.

T'ien T'ai Buddhist Doctrine

Buddhism first arrived in China around 50 CE. Over the next 300 years, many of the Buddha's teachings, which are called the *sutras*, were brought from India. As more and more of the sutras were translated into Chinese, it became very difficult for people to study and learn Buddhism—no one knew where to start. Some of the sutras taught simple doctrines that were easy to apply to one's life, while others taught complex, abstract doctrines. By the sixth century, there were so many sutras that seemed to contradict one another that not even the most educated sages could figure out which teachings were authentic and which teachings were of limited value. Fortunately, a Buddhist sage named T'ien T'ai (also known as Chih-i) decided to apply his wisdom to the problem.

T'ien T'ai systematized the Buddhist sutras and was able to reveal the greatest teachings of the Buddha. Based on his insights, the T'ien T'ai School of Buddhism was founded in China. T'ien T'ai took all the Buddhist sutras and categorized them based on when they were taught

during the life of the Buddha. One of his most famous systems for classifying the sutras is the Five Periods and the Eight Teachings.

The Five Periods are the Flower Garland (Kegon) period, the
Hīnayāna Collection (Āgama) period, the Great Extent (Hōdō) period,
the Wisdom (Hannya) period, and the Lotus-Nirvana (Hokke-Nehan)
period. The Flower Garland period includes the Buddha's teachings
during the first three weeks after the Buddha attained enlightenment.
The Hīnayāna Collection period includes the sutras taught during the
next twelve years; these are the sutras that Theravadan Buddhists use.
The Great Extent period includes many of the Mahāyāna sutras, particularly the early Mahāyāna teachings. The Wisdom period includes the
Heart Sutra and *Prajñāpāramitā Sutra*. The Lotus-Nirvana period
includes the *Lotus Sutra* and *Nirvana Sutra*. In this classification, the
most important sutra were those taught near the end of the Buddha's
life. Based on this system, the *Lotus Sutra* is the most important teaching, therefore T'ien T'ai based the doctrines of his school on that sutra.
He taught that all the teachings of the Buddha lead to the *Lotus Sutra*.
It is the pinnacle of the Buddha's teaching and is his most complete
teaching. The *Lotus Sutra* teaches doctrines that were not revealed in
earlier sutras.

The Supreme Teachings of the Lotus Sutra

Two particular doctrines in the *Lotus Sutra* are considered the most
important revelations in the sutra. These doctrines are that all beings,
no matter how defiled, can achieve enlightenment and that the Buddha
is eternally present in this universe.

In previous sutras, certain kinds of people were said not to have the
ability to obtain Buddhahood. These people were said to have
destroyed their ability to reach Buddhahood because of their
arrogance—they believed that they had already reached the highest
form of enlightenment possible. These practitioners were known as
śrāvakas and pratyekabuddhas. In the *Lotus Sutra*, the Buddha tells the
śrāvakas and pratyekabuddhas that they actually do have the ability to
attain Buddhahood. The Buddha also guarantees Buddhahood to many
monks, nuns, and lay-people. The *Lotus Sutra* was also the first sutra to
teach that women can reach enlightenment in their present form. Many
sutras taught that women could only reach enlightenment after being
reborn as men. In Chapter 12 of the *Lotus Sutra*, Devadatta is also guar-
anteed Buddhahood. Earlier during the Buddha's life Devadatta, who
was also the Buddha's cousin, had tried to kill the Buddha and had
caused disharmony among his followers. In previous sutras, Devadatta
was cast in the role of the enemy of Buddhism who had no chance of

ever attaining enlightenment because of his misdeeds. However, in the *Lotus Sutra* the Buddha said that even Devadatta would eventually reach Buddhahood. In the same chapter, the Dragon King's daughter reaches enlightenment. Not only is she a female, she is not even a human—in previous sutras this was as much an obstacle to enlightenment as being a woman. The *Lotus Sutra* teaches that that all beings have the ability to reach enlightenment in this very life, no matter what their apparent nature or obstacles may be.

Ichinen Sanzen

How is it possible that a person, no matter how evil or defiled, can become a Buddha in his or her current lifetime? Is it not necessary for an individual to spend lifetimes purifying his or her life? T'ien T'ai discovered a very important doctrine within the *Lotus Sutra* which explains that we all have Buddha nature within us; this is how we can attain Buddhahood in our present lifetimes. This teaching is called the Three Thousand Conditions in One Moment of Thought, or *ichinen sanzen*.

Ichinen sanzen is so profound that an entire book could be written about it, but here we will just cover the essentials of the concept. Essentially, it means that each moment of our life contains infinite potential, including the potential for Buddhahood. The number "three thousand" refers to a very specific way of looking at that infinite potential, which we will analyze here.

First, we start by considering the ten worlds. The state of one's life in general can be one of the ten worlds or "life conditions." The lowest of these is the state of hell. This is not a place below the earth where devils torture those who have been evil, but is a state of mind in this life. Here the world is nothing but gloom. For those who live in the condition of hell, the world is a place of agony and powerlessness. The next condition is that of the "Hungry Spirits." This is a world of unending desire for what one cannot possess. It is a state of profound greed and craving. In the next condition, the world of animals, the person's life is controlled by animal instincts. The next world is anger. Some people let anger rule their lives. They cause suffering to themselves and to others because of their anger. The next state is the world of humans. This is the condition of everyday life, where the most of humanity dwells on a daily basis. The next state, heaven, like hell at the beginning of the list, is not a place that one goes for eternity after death. Instead, it is that feeling we have when we are in a state of complete peace and contentment. It is a state of contentment such as when we we feel that our whole world is a perfect place to be, everything is just the way it should be, and nothing like suffering is on the horizon. These first six of the ten worlds are called the lower worlds. The six lower worlds describe the basic nature of most people's lives. The next two, mentioned a few paragraphs ago, are the worlds of the śrāvakas and pratyekabuddhas. These states describe those who have started on the path to buddhahood as people who are learning or those who have made realizations through individual practice. These two are different from the next level of the bodhisattva, because at these lower levels, the individual practices for his or her own enlightenment. The bodhisattva is also practicing for enlightenment, but not just for personal awakening. The bodhisattva practices so that all other beings may reach enlightenment. The highest level in the ten worlds is that of the Buddha. Buddha-mind is hard for us to reach in this world or even to imagine. The world of Buddhahood reflects infinite compassion and wisdom.

If you think about it, these conditions do not just describe the overall state of one's whole life. Each state can also arise in a person from moment to moment as the day goes by. A person whose life is generally characterized by anger also may experience moments of infinite compassion. A person who generally behaves as a bodhisattva may occasionally experience the frustrating, powerless feeling of the hell realm. Remember that these conditions are transitory. We can keep ourselves in one world or another for awhile, but usually we find that the condition will soon give away to another. Anger does not last. Even joy does not last.

To describe this, the formula for ichinen sanzen takes the ten worlds and multiplies them by the ten worlds again to make one hundred worlds. Each of these conditions contains all of the others in potential. As you think back on your day, you can probably see how some of these conditions have arisen in your own mind and how they have given way to other conditions after time.

In the next step, the one hundred worlds are multiplied by a set of ten aspects. These aspects are the components that come together to make everything that is real, whether it is a person, an animal, a thing, or an event. The Ten Aspects are listed in Chapter Two of the *Lotus Sutra*; in our daily practice, we chant the Ten Aspects as a part of the recitation of selected parts of the sutra:

> The reality of all things in regard to
> their appearances as such,
> their natures as such,
> their entities as such,
> their powers as such,
> their activities as such,
> their primary causes as such,
> their environmental causes as such,

their effects as such,
their rewards and retributions as such,
and their equality as such despite these differences.

Ten times the one hundred worlds makes one thousand conditions of life.

The final step in the formula for ichinen sanzen multiplies these conditions by the Three Factors. These are the aspects of ourselves and the world around us that play a part in the reality of our lives: individual characteristics, our society's characteristics, and characteristics of the world around us.

This brings us to the three thousand conditions that ichinen sanzen teaches are contained in one moment of thought. They change from moment to moment in our lives. Even our minds are constantly changing. If you just sit for a minute quietly right now, you will notice your mind thinking about all kinds of things. Your condition may change from one of interest to one of anger when someone disrupts your reading. You may find the exercise itself boring or even silly. However, the important thing that this theory reveals is that Buddha nature is contained in all these conditions. Likewise, Buddhahood itself contains all the others in itself. This shows that all beings have Buddha nature deep inside them. Buddha nature is like rich soil that has great potential to bring forth excellent fruit. Nonetheless, in order to make the fruit, you need not only the soil but also seeds, water, and sunshine. This is the function that our Buddhist practice serves. In Nichiren Buddhism, the *Lotus Sutra* and the Odaimoku are the seeds of Buddhahood that with careful practice will sprout and grow. Eventually the "sprout" will mature and the flower of enlightenment can bloom. A fuller explanation of this concept can be found in the Nichiren Buddhist Doctrine section below under the heading "The Buddhism of Sowing."

T'ien T'ai wrote many commentaries and theories about the Eternal Buddha, the *Lotus Sutra*, and our ability to be enlightened. T'ien T'ai's teachings made the practice of the *Lotus Sutra* widespread in China. In the eighth century, a man named Great Master Dengyō brought T'ien T'ai doctrine to Japan. It became one of the most popular forms of

---

Ichinen Sanzen in a Nutshell

The Ten Worlds
Hell, Hungry Spirits, Animals, Anger, Humanity, Heaven, Śrāvakas, Pratyekabuddhas, Bodhisattvas, and Buddhahood

multiplied by

The Ten Worlds
Hell, Hungry Spirits, Animals, Anger, Humanity, Heaven, Śrāvakas, Pratyekabuddhas, Bodhisattvas, and Buddhahood

multiplied by

The Ten Aspects
Appearance, Nature, Entity, Power, Activity, Primary Cause, Environmental Cause, Effect, Reward and Retribution, and Equality Despite Theses Differences

multiplied by

The Three Factors
Land, Other Beings, and Components of Self

Buddhism practiced in Japan during the Heian Period. It was known by the Japanese pronunciation of the founder's name, Tendai.

Just like all things, the cycle of birth, maturity, decline, and death affects the doctrines of Buddhism. Tendai Buddhism slowly lost its reigning status to other forms of Buddhism; slowly the practices of the Tendai school changed to compete with these other forms of Buddhism. The death of the Buddhism that T'ien T'ai taught was followed by the emergence of a magical form of Buddhism, Shingon. Tendai Buddhism adapted and absorbed many aspects of Shingon in an attempt to prevent its followers from being lured away. By the thirteenth century, Tendai Buddhism was so changed that it had little similarity to its original form.

Nichiren Buddhist Doctrine

It was at this time in Japan that Nichiren Shōnin, the founder of Nichiren Shu, appeared on the scene (see Chapter 4 for the story of Nichiren Shōnin's life). He revived the *Lotus Sutra* as the supreme teaching of the Eternal Buddha. Nichiren Shōnin studied all the different forms of Buddhism available to him and came to the conclusion that the *Lotus Sutra* was the ultimate teaching of the Buddha. By using the original teachings of the Tendai school and by listening to and studying all the forms of Buddhism, Nichiren Shōnin thrust the *Lotus Sutra* back into the sight of the people of his time.

Nichiren Shōnin taught the concept of ichinen sanzen, but he transformed the idea from an abstract philosophical theory into a practical teaching with meaning in one's daily life. Nichiren Shōnin realized that T'ien T'ai and Great Master Dengyō both were great teachers but had not disclosed all the teachings of the *Lotus Sutra*. They had held back some of the insights in the *Lotus Sutra* because the time for teaching those things had not yet arrived. Nichiren Shōnin, on the other hand, lived in the Declining Age of the Dharma. The Declining Age of the Dharma is a time period during which the original teachings of the Buddha are so remote in the past that their original meaning is lost and people fight amongst themselves because of that loss. It lasts from 2000 years after the death of the Buddha for hundreds of thousands of years in the future. The Declining Age of the Dharma is the time when the Bodhisattvas from Underground (see the summary of the *Lotus Sutra* in Chapter 7) have promised the Eternal Buddha that they will spread the *Lotus Sutra*. Nichiren Shōnin realized that he had received the Dharma from the Eternal Buddha and that it was his mission to spread the *Lotus*

Sutra in this time. He spent his life in fulfilling the promise of the Bodhisattvas from Underground.

The Three Great Hidden Dharmas

One of Nichiren Shōnin's most important teachings is the "Three Great Hidden Dharmas," or the *Sandaihihō*. They are:

> The Most Venerable One Revealed in the Essential Section of the *Lotus Sutra*.

> The Precepts Platform Prescribed in the Essential Section of the *Lotus Sutra*.

> The Odaimoku-chanting Founded in the Essential Section of the *Lotus Sutra*.

First, what is the Essential Section of the *Lotus Sutra*? The *Lotus Sutra* is often divided into different parts to help analyze its meaning. One of the most common methods of division is splitting it into the Provisional Section (or the *Shakumon*) and the Essential Section (or the *Honmon*). The Provisional Section contains theoretical teachings; these are important, but do not explicitly reveal the ultimate reality. The Buddha's most important teaching, in which the ultimate reality is explicitly revealed, is contained in the Essential Section of the *Lotus Sutra*.

So what is the "Most Venerable One," or *Honzon*, that is revealed in the *Lotus Sutra*? In the Essential Section of the sutra, Śākyamuni Buddha reveals that he is the original Buddha. He shows that his enlightened life extends from the distant past into the distant future. Since a closer look makes it clear that his enlightened life extends with-

out limit, we refer to Śākyamuni as the Eternal Buddha. He further reveals that he lives as the Eternal Buddha in this world; many other sutras talk about other Buddhas who live in great purified lands other than this world. The schools that follow these other sutras will often claim that one needs to be reborn in one of those pure lands to attain enlightenment because the Buddha is gone from this

A Representation of the Most Venerable One: the Eternal Śākyamuni Buddha surrounded by the leaders of the Bodhisattvas from Underground.

world. However, the *Lotus Sutra* reveals that we do not need to go to any other realm to become enlightened, because the pure land is right here in this world and the Buddha is eternal, always present in this world with us. Because of this, we will all eventually reach enlightenment just as the Buddha himself did. The Dharma always exists in this world. It does not vanish because the Buddha's physical body has passed away. The Eternal Buddha, the one who can lead us to enlightenment, is our Most Venerable One, or Honzon, the object of our devotion. We deeply respect and revere the Eternal Buddha as our teacher and our guide on the path to enlightenment. The Eternal Buddha Śākyamuni is represented with the four leaders of the Bodhisattvas from Underground, because these bodhisattvas appear in this time to lead people to the true Dharma of the *Lotus Sutra*.

The second hidden teaching is the "Precepts Platform," or *Kaidan*, of the Essential Section. When a Buddhist becomes a monk or a nun, he or she takes vows to follow the Buddha. These vows are taken at a place called a precepts platform. "Precepts" are standards of conduct. The precepts that one vows to uphold when becoming a monk or nun are similar to the precepts that are part of the Six Perfections discussed earlier. However, monks vow to uphold many more than only five precepts. Before the *Lotus Sutra*, the precepts and requirements that monks, nuns, and lay people had to fulfill as Buddhists were very different. The *Lotus Sutra* teaches that this is not a valid distinction. All who follow the *Lotus Sutra* are disciples of the Eternal Buddha who follow the example of the Bodhisattvas from Underground. Until Nichiren Shōnin revealed the truth within the *Lotus Sutra*, however, there was not a precepts platform based on this teaching, much less one that monks, nuns, and laypeople could all use. Nichiren Shōnin's teachings indicate that the precept platform can be anywhere one practices chanting Namu Myōhō Renge Kyō.

This leads us to the third hidden teaching: the Odaimoku Chanting revealed in the Essential Section of the *Lotus Sutra*. "Odaimoku" means "honored title" in Japanese. "Myōhō Renge Kyō" is the Chinese title of the *Lotus Sutra*. Within the Essential Section, Nichiren Shōnin found that this Odaimoku was a sparkling gem that could be used by all people in the Declining Age of the Dharma. This gem is Namu Myōhō Renge Kyō. "Namu" is derived from the Sanskrit word *namas*, which means "I give reverence or honor to..." so the whole phrase means "I Honor the *Lotus Sutra*." The Buddha took all of the teachings of the Dharma and condensed them into this simple phrase. By chanting Namu Myōhō Renge Kyō, we bring the merits of the Buddha into our lives and elevate our own life condition toward Buddhahood. Chanting the Odaimoku waters the seed of Buddhahood within us so that we slowly manifest enlightenment. However, the Odaimoku is also the seed of Buddhahood itself, and the fruits of Buddhahood as well. In the essay *Treatise on Spiritual Insight and the Most Venerable One*, Nichiren Shōnin writes, "Śākyamuni Buddha's practices and his enlightenment attained by his practices are contained in the five characters: Myō Hō Ren Ge Kyō. When we keep these five characters, we shall naturally be given the merits of the practices and enlightenment of the Buddha."

The Buddhism of Sowing Seeds of Buddhahood

Nichiren Buddhism is sometimes called "the Buddhism of Sowing." Buddhahood can be seen as the fruit of Buddhist practice. To obtain a fruit, one needs a seed, earth, water, and sunshine. The potential that all sentient beings have to become Buddhas, the Buddha-nature, is likened to the earth or ground from which the plant springs. Buddhist practice is seen as the water and sunshine that support the growth of the plant and bring it to maturity so that it can bear the fruit of Buddhahood. But where does the seed come from?

The *Lotus Sutra* says in Chapter Two, "The seed of Buddhahood comes from dependent origination." This means that the seed relies on some cause for its existence and origin. In Chapter Three, the sutra says, "Those who do not believe in this sutra, but slander it, will destroy the seeds of Buddhahood of all living beings of the world." So not only does the seed need to be planted, but it is also fragile enough that the wrong actions of a few can have negative effects on the seeds of many people.

Nichiren Shōnin said that the Eternal Buddha Śākyamuni planted the seed of Buddha in all beings in the timeless past. However, in the Declining Age of the Dharma, because many people slander the Buddha's teaching, the seeds of Buddhahood have been scorched so that they are unable to sprout and bear fruit. So we now need to have new seeds planted within us.

In the *Lotus Sutra*, the Buddha gave the Bodhisattvas from Underground the mission of spreading the sutra in the Declining Age of the Dharma after the Buddha's passing. Because the *Lotus Sutra* is able to bring new life to the seeds of Buddhahood, Nichiren Shōnin said that transmitting the sutra was like sowing the seed of Buddhahood to the people of this age.

Nichiren Shōnin himself was the leader of those who perform the action of sowing in the Declining Age of the Dharma. He said, "For twenty-eight years, from April 28, 1253 to December, 1280, I have done nothing but devote myself to spreading the chanting of Namu Myōhō Renge Kyō to all of the people of Japan. My compassion is like that of a mother trying to feed her baby." Nichiren Shōnin's mission was to lead the people in this age to the practice of chanting the Odaimoku and taking faith in the *Lotus Sutra*; in this way, they could reestablish their relationship with the Eternal Buddha. The seed of Buddhahood, expressed verbally by Namu Myōhō Renge Kyō, is received from the Eternal Buddha through Nichiren Shōnin.

Just as Nichiren Shōnin devoted his life to sowing the seeds of Buddhahood, he also took the example of Bodhisattva Never Despising in Chapter 20 of the *Lotus Sutra*. This bodhisattva was the Buddha Śākyamuni in a previous life who would preach the Dharma to those around him. Even when those people would not believe him and tried to abuse him, he would tell them, "I do not despise you because you will all practice the way and eventually become buddhas." So even though Nichiren Shōnin was planting the seeds of Buddhahood in people who had lost it, he never held those people in contempt. This was because he knew that by the simple act of planting the seed, he was assuring them that they would someday become Buddhas, and therefore were worthy of respect even before that happened.

Nichiren Shōnin also said that his followers should sow the seeds of Buddhism. Therefore as Nichiren Buddhists it is our mission to spread the Odaimoku to others while maintaining a sense of deep respect for them.

Receiving the Buddha's Merits

Another problem with understanding the Buddha's teaching in the Declining Age of the Dharma is that we are so distant from the Buddha in time that it is difficult for us to understand his teachings. The Buddha taught in a way that made sense to people who lived in the culture of his time. Our culture is far different, of course, with different pressures, ideas, and demands on our time and awareness. So how can we obtain merit through the Buddha's teachings?

In Chapter 16 of the *Lotus Sutra*, the Duration of the Life of the Tathāgata, the Buddha said, "I am the father of the world. I am saving all living beings from suffering." The group "all living beings" has to include those who live in an age when it is difficult to understand the doctrines he preached. In his *Treatise on Spiritual Insight and the Most Venerable One*, Nichiren Shōnin explained how the Buddha extends his salvation to us:

> For those who are incapable of understanding the truth of ichinen sanzen [see explanation above under T'ien T'ai Buddhist doctrine], Lord Śākyamuni Buddha, with his great compassion, wraps this jewel with the five characters of *myō, hō, ren, ge,* and *kyō* and hangs it around the neck of the ignorant in the Declining Age of the Dharma. [*Writings of Nichiren Shōnin: Doctrine 2*, p. 164]

In the same treatise, Nichiren Shōnin also said

... Śākyamuni Buddha's merit of practicing the bodhisattva way leading to Buddhahood, as well as that of preaching and saving all living beings since his attainment of Buddhahood, are altogether contained in the five words of *myō, hō, ren, ge,* and *kyō*. Consequently, when we uphold the five words, the merits which he accumulated before and after his attainment of Buddhahood are naturally transferred to us. [Ibid., p. 146]

The Buddha, therefore, encapsulated all of the merits of his wisdom in the *Lotus Sutra*—specifically in the Odaimoku—so that we could receive its merits even without understanding the full truth of ichinen sanzen. This is known as the "Natural Transfer" of the Buddha's merits.

Without understanding, how can the merits of the Buddha's wisdom be transferred to us? In the sutra, the Buddha said, "They will be able to understand [this sutra] by faith." The transfer of merit from the Odaimoku is based simply on faith, not on intellectual understanding. Note that this is not "blind faith" as it is sometimes understood in Western culture; instead, it is initial trust that allows us to move to a point at which we see the truth of the *Lotus Sutra* for ourselves.

In the Declining Age of the Dharma, it is most important that we maintain our faith even when our wisdom falters so that we can continue to walk on the path of the Buddha's Dharma.

Nichiren Shu Doctrines in Practice

All of these doctrines come together to form the basic teachings of Nichiren Shu. The *Lotus Sutra* is the keystone of Buddhism, but even the very earliest Theravadan teachings, when seen in the light of the *Lotus Sutra*, have meaning to us as Buddhists. The only remaining thing to be explained is how these doctrines translate into our actions in our daily life.

Faith in Nichiren Buddhism and the *Lotus Sutra* begins within our minds. But if we are actually to live as Nichiren Buddhists, as opposed to simply paying lip service to Nichiren Buddhist beliefs, our faith will influence our actions and the way that we interact with the community. We cannot simply express our faith verbally by chanting the Odaimoku. Our faith must extend to the Three Kinds of Action: bodily action, verbal action, and mental action.

In other words, we should not simply praise the sutra with our lips by chanting Namu Myōhō Renge Kyō, but we must practice the sutra with our bodies and minds as well. Nichiren Shōnin is our example in this practice; he lived following the example of the bodhisattvas described in the *Lotus Sutra*.

The basic points of expressing our faith in our daily lives are explained in the Nichiren Shu creed:

1. We base our life on the example of the *Lotus Sutra* as personally experienced by Nichiren Shōnin.

2. We put our faith in the Eternal Buddha Śākyamuni, who is the true teacher of wisdom and compassion for all people.

3. We train ourselves to attain Buddhahood by upholding Namu Myōhō Renge Kyō, both in action and in spirit.

4. Our teacher is Nichiren Shōnin, who vowed to cultivate the Buddha nature of all people and create the land of the Buddha in this world. We also vow to work for that goal.

5. We are all the Buddha's children, and we will live together peacefully with all people in our search for the Truth.

As Nichiren Shu Buddhists, we should follow these guidelines to express the doctrines of Nichiren Buddhism through the Three Kinds of Action. Besides striving to perform our daily practice consistently (see Chapter 8) and participating in special ceremonies (Chapter 9), Buddhism calls for us to reflect our beliefs in our family life, in our workplace, and in our dealings with society. The Nichiren Shu recognizes certain basic truths that our daily lives should express in our actions. These truths, described in the following paragraphs, should naturally arise from our Buddhist practice; that is, we should live this way not because we are supposed to follow some rules, but because they express our natural beliefs.

Because all human beings have the potential to become Buddhas—their lives contain the world of Buddhahood because of ichinen sanzen—we should treat all other people as we wish to be treated ourselves. We should keep in mind the lesson of Bodhisattva Never Despise in Chapter Twenty of the *Lotus Sutra* (see Chapter 7 of this book for his story) who told everyone that he met that he respected them because they would become Buddhas one day. It is important not to judge people by their beauty, wealth, or fame, but rather to respect those who are compassionate, generous, and live lives that express the teachings of the Buddha.

Every person experiences both joy and suffering in life, so we should be compassionate with others. It is easy for us to say that we are happy for someone's success or sorry for their misfortune, but we should actually feel these words in our hearts as we say them. When we feel true compassion, our words and actions will affect other people and serve to increase their joy or lessen their pain. When this happens, we will make this world the Buddha's pure land, not only in deepest truth but in a way that can be seen by all people.

Just as we should be compassionate with others because we all have joy and suffering, we should be compassionate with ourselves by continuing to strive mindfully when difficulties arise in our own lives. Both joy and suffering are facts of life, and both are temporary. Nothing can be achieved if we are satisfied with fleeting success or if we are stopped by obstacles in our path. As both are sure to pass away after time, it is even more tragic to stop moving forward because of something impermanent.

The center of most people's lives is their family, whether by birth, marriage, or choice. Therefore, it is very important that we pay special attention to expressing compassion and trust within our families. Because of the complications of love and continuous contact, sometimes people actually end up being less caring and honest with their families than they are with other people. This is like building a house with a fortified second story while the first story and foundation are built from twigs and tarpaper. We must strive to be respectful, honest, and compassionate with our families—and we must also be sure to extend those same qualities to those outside of our families.

"Progress diligently," were the last words of the Buddha. As Buddhists, we must strive to progress in our faith, practice, and actions every day. In this way, the future will be better than the past. We should work so that mistakes we have made in the past are not repeated, and so that beneficial things that we have missed will become a part of our lives. This spirit should be applied within ourselves, between our family and friends, and in our careers. We should work for unashamed honesty, boundless compassion, and a deep-rooted respect for all things.

The most important goal of any belief is the improvement of self and of the world in general. As a meaningful Buddhist group, Nichiren Shu and its practitioners must strive for the peace, happiness, and enlightenment of every living thing. Human life and the environment must be cherished and protected, and society must be encouraged toward peace and happiness. Therefore, the Nichiren Shu firmly holds the convictions of opposition to all war, prohibition of nuclear arms, and justice and peace in society. Besides promoting these values in society, we believe that by living as the Buddha taught us in the *Lotus Sutra* and by following the teachings of Nichiren Shōnin, we can manifest these values naturally. We also spread this peace and happiness through the world by teaching others to follow the Buddha's teachings.

This is just a brief outline of the teachings of Nichiren Shu. The doctrines when examined in depth can be overwhelming and difficult. This is why we need the Saṅgha, or the community of those who follow the Buddha's teachings. In the Saṅgha, we grow and help each other in our practice and study. We have covered the basics of doctrine here, but one must be aware that the most important part of Buddhism is practice. You can read everything there is to read about Buddhism, but without practice you cannot understand it. On the other hand, even if you do not study and memorize all the Buddha's teachings, just chanting the Odaimoku will assure you of enlightenment.

Chapter 3
The Life of the Buddha

Around 500 BCE, tradition says on April 8th, a son was born to the king of a small northern Indian tribe ruled by the Śākya clan. As was the tradition at that time, King Śuddhodana and Queen Māyā of the Śākyas consulted seers to learn their child's destiny in life. Two possibilities were revealed to them. The first was that their new son might become a great conqueror, the ruler of all India—for what more could an ambitious father ask? However, to King Śuddhodana's dismay, the second was that his son might become a great sage, divorced from worldly things. The fact that this prophecy included the promise that his son might come to be the greatest teacher of all time did not make this any more desirable to a man of the king's temperament. He wanted his son to become the world's greatest ruler, not the world's greatest philosopher.

To steer his son away from a life of contemplation, the king ordered that Siddhārtha Gautama should live a life of pure comfort, never coming into contact with the sufferings of humankind. All through his youth, Siddhārtha was surrounded by luxury and by beautiful people, leading a life of ease. However, as young Siddhārtha grew into adolescence, he naturally grew curious and daring. He wished to see his kingdom and the world, and his father's desire that he remain secluded in palaces of pleasure only added spice to the adventure of going out into the world. The prince somehow convinced his charioteer to indulge him in his brief escapes to see his kingdom.

While the prince prepared to make his adventures in the world, court life among the Gautama clan continued apace. Prince Siddhārtha was married to a famously beautiful princess named Yaśodharā, and in the course of time, she fell pregnant with his child.

However, during his wife's pregnancy, Siddhārtha was venturing at last into the world as it really is. Having been confined in luxurious palaces in which no one but beautiful, young, healthy people were allowed, the young prince was in for some revelations as to the true nature of life. Siddhārtha's experience of coming to understand human suffering has been passed down through history as the story of the four sightings.

On one of Prince Siddhārtha's first journeys in his chariot, he came upon a decrepit old man, ravaged by the passage of time. Stunned that a person could be so stricken, the prince asked his charioteer what was wrong with this man. His charioteer explained that the man was old, and explained the nature of aging. Taken aback by this new-found knowledge, the prince asked his charioteer if this was unique to the old man or a few like him, or if all people were destined to become old. The charioteer replied, "This comes to us all."

The prince's next sighting was of a man overtaken by sickness. Again, Siddhārtha could not imagine that a person should suffer in such a way. Once again, the charioteer explained the matter to the prince, and told him that "This comes to us all."

The third sighting was of a corpse. The dead person's family and friends surrounded the body and mourned pitifully. We can imagine Siddhārtha's confusion: "Does the man sleep? Why are his friends so sad? Why does he not awaken to their cries of grief?" The charioteer explained to the prince that the man was dead: he lived no more, was lost to the world, and his family and friends grieved that he was lost to them. Siddhārtha was struck with a thought. "And my family, my friends, even myself, shall we all come to live no more?" The charioteer replied, "This comes to us all."

We can only imagine how troubled and bewildered Prince Siddhārtha was by these experiences. This young man in his mid-twenties for the first time in his life realized that people—including his companions, friends, family, wife, his coming son, and even himself—were subject to sickness, old age, and death. Shaken to the core, he no doubt wondered how he could ever hope to come to terms with these new concepts. Nonetheless, in his shock and confusion, he made yet another trip with his charioteer outside the palace. The prince's fourth sighting was of a wandering contemplative. His charioteer explained that this was a man who had left ordinary life to find peace and transcend the suffering of life. It all became clear in a flash: this was the path that Prince Siddhārtha must take. Despite his father's attempts to forestall such an outcome, the prince now determined that he too would become a wanderer and seek to conquer suffering. He saw that the conquest of kingdoms was of little moment compared to the conquest of the suffering of all people.

Upon his return to the palace from this trip, Siddhārtha was greeted with the news that his wife had born him a son. This did not dissuade him from his newfound path—in fact, he realized that his son's birth tempted him to put aside his plans, so he immediately named his son Rāhula, which means "fetter." Deep in the night, the prince stole away from the palace to start his life as a monk seeking to free all mankind from the fetters of suffering.

Siddhārtha, upon leaving his home and the sheltered life to which he had become accustomed, first sought learning under the guidance of recognized masters of the contemplative life. He sought out a well known guru, but within a short time he had mastered this master's teachings. His preceptor, stunned at Siddhārtha's rapid progress, acknowledged that he had no more to teach the former prince. He offered Siddhārtha the chance to become fellow leader of his school. However, Siddhārtha was not satisfied with the level of achievement that he had reached—he chose to seek a deeper level of understanding.

Siddhārtha quickly found another guru who had attained a higher level of understanding. Once again, however, he quickly mastered everything that the sage had to teach him. This teacher also offered the former prince the position of leader of his school. Again, he found that the teaching did not lead to the perfect peace he sought.

When he decided to leave this school, five of the other students chose to leave with him. Together, they would seek the ultimate truth that surpassed the teachings they had so far encountered.

These six seekers after the truth submerged themselves into self-improvement. The method that they chose was the one that many have attempted in seeking ultimate truth: self-denial and total asceticism. For six years, Siddhārtha and his companions denied themselves every comfort and subsisted on the sparsest of diets. At times, the former prince's meal would be a single grain of rice. He became so emaciated that he nearly starved to death. These exercises in asceticism left him so exhausted that he would faint in weakness even if he only tried to answer the call of nature. Finally, in attempting to bathe in a river, he nearly drowned when he found he no longer had the energy to return to the shore. Somehow, Siddhārtha managed to pull himself back to shore where he promptly fell face down, unable to move from his exertions. In this state, Sujāta, the daughter of a lowly herder, found him and saved his life by offering him some meager gruel.

This is when Siddhārtha realized that asceticism was not the path to the truth. Like his study under the gurus, the practices of self-denial allowed one to see the final goal vaguely in the distance, but did not move one any nearer to the truth. How could a body that was too malnourished even to allow one to fulfill the simple act of urination provide sufficient nourishment to allow the mind to achieve the ultimate goal? Certainly it would prove impossible; the soon-to-be Buddha returned to eating enough to maintain his bodily health, but did not indulge himself beyond the requirements of keeping his strength and mind intact. When his health was restored, he retired to a park near Uruvela in which he frequently meditated. He sat beneath what is now known, in memory of the coming events, as the "Bodhi tree," a variety of fig. He resolved to sit there in meditation until he had awakened to the highest truth. At this point, his five fellow-seekers came upon him and recognized him from afar. They also recognized the fact that he had given up asceticism. Disappointed by what they saw, they assumed that Siddhārtha had given up the path to enlightenment and went away without meeting him, greatly disillusioned by what they perceived to be the failure of a promising sage.

The stories vary as to how long Siddhārtha remained under this tree in meditation. Some say that he sat for three days, some say that he sat in this place in meditation frequently and that the subsequent events came to pass in due time, others claim that his realization occurred "that night." Whatever the case may be, one evening he sat in meditation under the Bodhi tree, and the final pieces in the puzzle of the universe fell into place during the ensuing night.

Tradition tells us that on that night Siddhārtha encountered the hosts of Māra, the "Evil One," or the essence of fundamental darkness and ignorance. However, this is no evil spirit such as the devils of Western religion; instead, Māra is a personification of the negative forces within each of us that prevent us from realizing the perfect truth. Truly, they are legion: Attavāda, or egoism, which tempts us to seek gain only for ourselves; Viśikitcha, or doubt, which tempts us to believe that our efforts are in vain; Kāma, or passion, which tempt us to live for the pleasure of the moment; and many others like hatred, desire for fame, self-righteousness, pride, and ignorance. However, by the time a quarter of the night had passed, Siddhārtha had overcome his inner demons. His own doubts, prejudices, and negativities could no longer restrain him.

Having overcome these internal obstacles, the future Buddha passed into a state of meditation so profound that he became aware of his previous lifetimes. That is to say, he realized the law of cause and effect, or karma, that regulates the entire universe. Simply stated, this law tells us that for every action there is a reaction. If you wish to understand why things are as they are now, simply look at the causes that set them in motion in the past. To see what will be in the future, look to the causes being made in the present.

During the next phase of the night, Siddhārtha's awareness encompassed the workings of the universe as a whole. He perceived the laws that regulate the universe and saw that every thing is dependent for its conditions, form, and even existence upon every other thing. Nothing in the universe is independent or isolated from any other thing. In this way, the deepest workings of all phenomena were revealed to this man who had been sheltered from the most basic facts of life early in his manhood.

Finally, in the last watch of the night as the sun threatened to break above the horizon, Siddhārtha's consciousness came to encompass the highest truth: every reality became known to him, he became fully awake to the truth, and he discerned the reasons for, causes of, and most importantly, the path to ending suffering. He was now fully enlightened and was the Buddha, the Awakened One.

The Buddha meditated on his realization for seven days following his enlightenment. After this period of rest and reflection, he arose planning to proclaim the truth that he had discovered. However, Māra the Tempter (or whatever was left of Siddhārtha's inner weaknesses) made one more attempt to sidetrack the Buddha. In this attack, all of the darkest workings of the human mind made one final combined attack—doubt, selfishness, pride, and all the rest. "Now that you have attained Nirvana, why go any further? The common people will be unable to understand the truth that you would teach them. You have attained the goal you sought; why do you not simply pass into the perfect stillness of death right away? Attempting to teach those who are comfortable with their illusions will be tiring and frustrating. Is this the state sought by he who has understood perfect inner peace?" Of course, such arguments did not sway the Buddha. In his compassion, he chose to teach his truth to all so that all living beings could escape the effects of suffering.

After his enlightenment, Siddhārtha was known as the "Buddha," or the "Awakened One." He was also given the name "Śākyamuni," which means "Sage of the Śākya Clan." Śākyamuni Buddha said that he had attained Nirvana. The Buddha said that this state could not be described in words, nor truly understood by any who had not yet experienced it. However, since the goal of the Buddha was to enable all living beings to attain this state, he did convey some idea of what it was like without necessarily defining it. The word "nirvana" means to be extinguished, like a candle flame being snuffed out. Nirvana is the extinguishing of the flame that leads to suffering within our lives and an end to the cycle that leads us on the roller coaster ride of alternating pain and pleasure. Nirvana is not some otherworldly paradise; the Buddha experienced Nirvana in this world. Furthermore, his experience in this world after achieving nirvana was not without its trials; some of his experiences certainly seem to be the sorts of things that would cause suffering. However, Nirvana is not a change in the events of one's life, it is instead a change in how one perceives and is affected by those events. It is the state in which one's happiness is not dependent upon outside events, in which one is not made to suffer by the simple realities of existence. It should be noted that nirvana also does not mean extinguishment as in death; another word, *parinirvāṇa*, is used to describe the state of an enlightened being when his or her physical body dies.

After his enlightenment, the Buddha first taught the five companions he had been traveling with before he gave up asceticism. These five had seen Siddhārtha as he sat under the Bodhi Tree and had considered him lost to the way of contemplation because they could see that he was no longer practicing asceticism. As a result, they were prejudiced against him and, seeing him coming toward them from a distance, agreed to withhold respectful greeting from him. On his approach, however, they immediately recognized that he was, at the very least, worthy of respect and so rose to greet him. After only a few words, his presence, peacefulness, and obvious awareness convinced them that he had indeed attained the highest awakening. So to these five lucky seekers, the Buddha first preached his way. This is known as the "First Turning of the Wheel of the Dharma," *Dharma* being the word used to describe his teaching. In this teaching, Śākyamuni expounded the core doctrines of Buddhism. These basic teachings of Buddhism are explained in the first half of Chapter 2. The five wise men immediately recognized how profound the Buddha's teachings were, and so vowed to follow his path, the Buddha Dharma. They became the first monks in the Buddhist Saṅgha (*saṅgha* means assembly and is the word used for the followers of the Buddha).

The Buddha's teachings profoundly affected all those who heard him preach. Soon, several thousands of people had joined the Saṅgha as monks. Many of these were able, through the teaching of the Buddha, to achieve a state of enlightenment for themselves; such people where called arhats. Lay people also began to follow the Buddha Dharma. As the Saṅgha grew in size, the Buddha gave many lectures and sermons about the Dharma and suggested rules for the Saṅgha to help it continue to thrive. At that time, such teachings were preserved in oral form only—the teachings were not written down until over 100 years after the Buddha himself died. The sermons and lectures were collected into "sutras," which form the basic body of the Buddha's teachings as we have received them today. The rules for the order of monks and nuns were collected in the "Vinaya" (the rules for laypeople were taught in the sutras). The final part of the written collection is the "Abidharma," which is an analysis of the teachings in the sutras.

The Buddha wandered, taught, and converted many people for some 40 years after his enlightenment. Thousands of sutras reveal that he taught everyone he met: ascetics and those who loved pleasure, beggars and kings, farmers and warriors, those who agreed with him and those who came to him expecting to defeat him in debate. As he entered old age, many of the inhabitants of the lands through which he wandered had accepted the Buddha Dharma as the path to the ultimate truth.

In his eightieth year, the Buddha finally came to the end of his life. Having spent most of his life teaching others that all things are impermanent, he and those who had grasped his teachings were well aware that the person of the Buddha would eventually cease to be. In a grove of Sal Trees in Kuśinigara, the Buddha laid down in his final hours. He called his closest followers to him for final words, assuring all that he had not held any teachings back, that his teachings were complete and thorough and able to lead all living beings from suffering. Those of his followers who were still having trouble accepting the idea of impermanence, particularly when it came to their beloved teacher, he reassured and admonished. He reminded them that all things are indeed impermanent; to be able to abide the unsatisfactory nature of reality was their goal. Finally, in the night of February 15th, the Buddha spoke the words, "Make yourself your guiding light; rely on yourself instead of on others. Make the Dharma your guiding light; rely on the Dharma instead of on others." After passing

Kuśinigara, the place where the Buddha died.

through several states of incredibly high awareness, the Buddha passed away and attained *parinirvāṇa*, the state of final extinction.

Chapter 4
Life of Nichiren Shonin

The Early Years

Nichiren Shōnin was born on February 16, 1222 in the small fishing village of Kominato on the east coast of Japan. Kominato was a remote village whose people suffered the hardships common to the simple and poor in medieval times. Indeed, Nichiren's parents, Shigetada Jirō Nukina and his wife Umegiku, were considered to be very lowly since Shigetada made his living by fishing—those whose jobs required the taking of life were called *sendara*, the lowest social class. The simplicity of his home village and the low class of his parents would later strongly influence Nichiren Shōnin's views on society and life's suffering.

Traditional stories tell us that Umegiku had a dream that the sun riding atop a lotus blossom descended into her body when Nichiren was conceived. When the child was born, legend also tells us that a clear spring appeared in his parents' garden and lotus flowers blossomed in the winter water of the village's bay. His parents named their son Zennichi-maro.

A bright child, his father sent him to Seichōji, the local Buddhist temple at Mount Kiyosumi, to receive an education when he was eleven. This was rare for a child of the lower classes, but his quick and questioning mind attracted the attention of Dōzen-bo. In fact, such attention was so rare for the child of a fisherman that some scholars think that perhaps Shigetada had been a samurai, but had retired to become a fisherman. In either case, Zennichi-maro was fortunate to receive an education beginning at an early age.

After four years of diligent study, Zennichi-maro was ordained as a Buddhist priest and given his religious name, Renchō. During his training, Renchō had begun to wonder why there were ten different sects of Buddhism that all claimed to possess the true teaching of the Buddha when the Buddha himself had only taught one school of Buddhism. Determined to solve this mystery and uncover the Buddha's true teachings, Renchō decided to study with great concentration to find the answer.

After a year of diligent study, however, Renchō found that he was no closer to his answer. Frustrated and confused, he went to the shrine of Bodhisattva Kokūzō (Ākāśagarbha) at Seichōji and prayed to become the wisest man in Japan. After 21 days in profound meditation, Renchō had a vision that the bodhisattva had granted him a "Precious Jewel of Wisdom" that would enable him to discover the true teachings of the Buddha.

Realizing that he had exhausted the resources of Seichōji, Renchō requested permission to further his studies at other temples. Dōzen-bo knew that Renchō's potential required more than Seichōji could give him, so the old master gave the young priest permission to take his studies elsewhere.

Advancing Studies

Renchō first traveled to Kamakura, the military capital of Japan at that time. He spent a long time studying at Buddhist schools in the capital to broaden his knowledge. When he had studied everything that Kamakura had to offer, he returned to Seichōji.

Four years had passed since he left his home town. Both his parents and Dōzen-bo were happy to see Renchō return. Because of the young priest's advanced study in Kamakura, Dōzen-bo hoped that he now might begin to train Renchō to take over his place as head of Seichōji. However, Renchō had returned to ask for leave to travel even further abroad for even deeper study. Renchō asked Dōzen-bo for permission to travel to Kyōto, the imperial capital of Japan, where the center of Buddhist learning was at that time on Mount Hiei. Dōzen-bo knew that Renchō had to further his studies—Renchō had submitted an essay to Dōzen-bo indicating that he believed that the highest teaching of the Buddha might be found in the *Lotus Sutra*. Though disturbed by the idea because he was a traditionalist, Dōzen-bo recognized that Renchō had to pursue his learning further. He gave permission for Renchō to travel to Kyōto.

Near Kyōto is the temple complex of Mount Hiei. Founded by the Great Master Dengyō in the Eighth Century, in Renchō's time the Mount Hiei complex was the center of Buddhism in Japan. Monks from every school of Buddhism studied there, and the library contained a copy of every Buddhist text in Japan. Great Master Dengyō (also known as Saichō) introduced the Tendai school of Buddhism to Japan based on the T'ien T'ai school of China. This school originally taught that the *Lotus Sutra* is the highest of the Buddha's teachings and that Śākyamuni (the historical Buddha) is the Buddha of this world and its inhabitants. However, in the time since the founding of Mount Hiei, Great Master Dengyō's teachings had been diluted by the teachings of the esoteric school of Buddhism, Shingon.

Shortly after Renchō arrived at Mount Hiei, he met one of its most respected teachers, Master Shumpan. Recognizing the advanced learning of Renchō, Master Shumpan took the new student under his wing as a student. Advancing in his studies rapidly, Renchō was put in charge of the Students' Hall after a short time.

Renchō's main task was to review all of the Buddhist scriptures. However, he did not simply read without questioning. The *Nirvana Sutra*, considered to be the last sutra preached by the Buddha before he died, set out four guidelines for judging the truth of any teaching. Renchō considered his awareness of these guidelines to be one of the fruits of the wisdom that Bodhisattva Kokūzō had given him. These guidelines are: (1) to rely upon the Dharma, not upon persons; (2) to rely on the meaning, not on the words alone; (3) to rely on

Yokawa Joko-in, the temple at the location of Nichiren Shōnin's place of study while at Mount Hiei.

wisdom, not on knowledge alone; and (4) to rely on sutras that reveal the whole truth, not on sutras that only reveal partial truth.

For several years, Renchō remained at Mount Hiei in deep study of Buddhism. He was exposed to the practices of many different schools of Buddhism. The practitioners of these schools also participated in a common activity at Mount Hiei—doctrinal debate. Two monks with opposing viewpoints would come together and conduct an intellectual debate on the merits of their views with many of the other priests and monks watching. Sometimes the observers would also question the debaters. In this way, Renchō was also exposed to the doctrinal thought of many advanced students of Buddhism. Most importantly, Renchō read through the entire body of Buddhist scripture at Mount Hiei. Finally, having experienced Buddhism of every kind to its fullest and having studied the innermost depths of Buddhist doctrine, Renchō felt that he had discovered the true teaching of the Buddha. The highest teaching was to be found in the *Lotus Sutra*, which revealed that Śākyamuni Buddha was the true Buddhist teacher for this world since the infinite past.

However, though his belief was firm, Renchō did not simply take his newfound wisdom for granted. First he would test his new belief. The first trial was by debate at Mount Hiei. With many learned monks and priests arguing against him, Renchō defended his idea that the *Lotus Sutra* was superior to all of the other teachings. Despite the large number of knowledgeable opponents, Renchō succeeded in winning the debate. No one was able to show that his conclusions were incorrect.

Renchō left Mount Hiei and spent time at many of the other grand temples in and around Kyōto searching for an idea, argument, or Buddhist insight that might undermine his insight into Buddhism. He could find none. It was time for him to proclaim his profound insight at his first sermon.

Proclaiming the Truth

Renchō's first audience for proclaiming the truth he discovered would be at the temple where he first studied Buddhism, Seichōji. He returned to the temple, paid his respects to Dōzen-bo, and went into the forest for a week-long purification retreat to prepare for his announcement. On the final day of this retreat, April 28, 1253, Renchō awoke before sunrise and climbed to the top of Mount Kiyosumi to face the sun as it rose over the Pacific Ocean. As the sun broke into view, he chanted "Namu Myōhō Renge Kyō," proclaiming to the world the truth of his awakening for the first time. (For the significance of this phrase, the Odaimoku, please see Chapter 2 in this book.) As he made ready to spread the true teaching of the Buddha within the *Lotus Sutra*, Renchō embraced a new name: Nichiren. His new name, which means "Sun Lotus," symbolized his teaching—like the sun, the teaching of the *Lotus Sutra* enlightens all that it shines upon, and like the lotus flower, which produces pure white blossoms even growing out of a muddy swamp.

Nichiren Shōnin traveled down Mount Kiyosumi to the temple and delivered his message to the people who had gathered for the event. Besides Dōzen-bo and the other priests of the temple, some local lay persons were also there, including the ruling lord of the area, Kagenobu Tōjō. Everyone there was a believer in Pure Land Buddhism; they expected that Nichiren Shōnin would deliver a sermon to them about the saving power of the Buddha of the Pure Land, Amida, who they believed would bring them to a heaven-like realm after death. Much to their surprise—and anger in many cases—Nichiren Shōnin instead delivered a speech criticizing Pure Land Buddhism as being completely against the teaching of the real Buddha. He further explained that the *Lotus Sutra* was the true teaching for this world, and that the original Buddha, Śākyamuni, should be the most respected object of Buddhist devotion, and the Pure Land's Amida was not to be prayed to like some kind of god. Amida, according to the *Lotus Sutra*, was only an expedient symbol that Śākyamuni Buddha used to help lead certain kinds of believers to the final truth. Finally, Nichiren Shōnin declared that the correct practice for this time and world was chanting the Odaimoku, and that praying to Amida Buddha by chanting his name would only lead to suffering and hellish states.

Seichōji: Hall Commemorating Nichiren Shōnin.

The Pure Land Buddhists were not impressed; though a few weighed Nichiren Shōnin's words, most were angered. Indeed, Kagenobu Tōjō almost immediately called for Nichiren's arrest and execution as a heretic. However, despite his dismay and confusion at his former student's apparently heretical speech, Dōzen-bo instructed several of the other priests to help Nichiren escape from Mount Kiyosumi by a secret path.

Nichiren Shōnin was quickly taken to a temple outside of Kagenobu Tōjō's range of power, Renge-ji. However, it was not part of Nichiren's plan to hide himself away; he must spread news of his revelation to all the people of Japan so they could practice Buddhism correctly. Japan was undergoing a time of hardship and suffering. The government was unstable and there was frequent bloodshed as different factions attempted to gain control. Plagues, famines, and natural disasters seemed to occur far more frequently than ever before. Nichiren Shōnin believed that the disorder and suffering was a result of the loss of the Buddha's true teaching. The incorrect and heretical practices of the Pure Land, esoteric, and Zen schools were a direct cause of the misfortune of the people and the country. He could help save Japan and its people only if he preached the truth to which he had awakened and convert the people back to the true Buddhist teachings of Śākyamuni.

So, instead of staying in the relative safety and seclusion of Renge-ji temple, Nichiren Shōnin soon left and traveled through some of the more rural provinces of Japan, preaching his beliefs to the rulers of these backwater places. Often, the lords of these regions had been sent to regions remote from the centers of power because they did not approve of the government or had suffered political setbacks. Some others preferred the distant provinces because they had more freedom,

being far away from the watchful eyes of their overlords. In these politically deprived and independent lords, Nichiren Shōnin found his first
converts.

Still, if he was to spread his teaching among all the people of Japan,
Nichiren Shōnin could not remain in the distant provinces. Encouraged
by the converts he had now won, he returned to the military capital,
Kamakura, hoping to convert more people and to persuade the government to recognize the truth of his claims.

The *Risshō Ankoku Ron*

He returned to a capital that was more than ever torn apart by the
instability of the government and the political maneuvering of those
who wanted more power. However, Nichiren Shōnin knew that things
would only get worse without his teaching, so he fearlessly began to
preach on the dangerous and chaotic streets of Kamakura. Often, he
was reviled and pelted with garbage by those who resented his challenge to their belief in Pure Land Buddhism. However, some of those
who heard him listened and were persuaded by his arguments, including some samurai. He also gained converts among other Buddhist
priests. The first of these was a friend of his from his days of study at
Mount Hiei, who became known as Nisshō. Another was a young
novice who took the name Nichirō. This young priest would come to be
one of Nichiren Shōnin's most devoted disciples. Together, they would
take to the streets, preach the truth of the *Lotus Sutra*, and chant the
Odaimoku in an attempt to convert more people and help save Japan.

Then, disaster struck. A series of enormous earthquakes hit Japan,
destroying the homes and lives of both wealthy and poor. Tidal waves
torn from the sea destroyed seaside settlements. Famine and disease
killed many people. Many comets and meteors appeared in the sky,
frightening the people who believed that these were ominous warnings
from the heavenly beings.

In East Asian cultures at that time, people expected the government
to save them from every kind of disaster; not just by preventing social
strife through stable government and by providing relief after catastrophes, but also by preventing natural disasters with official religious
ritual. So far, none of the high government officials had listened to
Nichiren Shōnin, so the government's response to the tragedies was to
perform esoteric Buddhist rituals. Much to Nichiren Shōnin's horror,
they were doing the very things that he had warned would cause disaster instead of avert it!

Nichiren Shōnin realized that his street sermons alone were not reaching some important people—the government ministers. While the common people were very important to Nichiren Shōnin, in Japanese society at that time the government performed the religious rites for the benefit of all the people, and often even sanctioned or outlawed personal religious practice. So Nichiren Shōnin secluded himself at the library in the Buddhist temple Jissō-ji in Iwamoto and began to work on an essay to submit to the government. In it, he would explain his reasoning and offer proof from the Buddhist scriptures. He hoped to convince the government to base their prayers and rituals for the good of the Japanese people on Śākyamuni's teaching in the *Lotus Sutra*.

It should be kept in mind that at this time, Nichiren Shōnin did not see himself as creating a new school of Buddhism. Instead, he was working to restore Tendai Buddhism to its original purity. He also believed that this purified Tendai Buddhism should be accepted as the one true practice for saving the Japanese people from suffering.

The title of this essay was *Risshō Ankoku Ron*, in English the *Treatise on Spreading Peace throughout the Country by Establishing the True Dharma*. It is written as a conversation between two people, a traveler and the Master. In the beginning, the traveler speaks of the catastrophes in Japan and the suffering of all the Japanese people. He wonders, with all of the sects of Buddhism in the country that are supposed to save the people from suffering, why Japan is suffering so many misfortunes. The Master explains the reasons he thinks this is so—Nichiren Shōnin's reasons—and offers a remedy—Nichiren Shōnin's remedy of worshiping the Eternal Śākyamuni Buddha of the *Lotus Sutra*. At first the traveler, who represents a typical believer in the muddled Buddhism of that time in Japan, is angered by the Master's statements. However, the Master gives his reasoning with passages from the scriptures, and at the end of the essay the traveler is convinced of the truth of the Master's statements.

On July 16, 1260, Nichiren Shōnin submitted the *Risshō Ankoku Ron* to Tokiyori Hōjō. Officially, Tokiyori was the retired ruler of the military government who had given up power to become a Buddhist priest; in reality, he was still the most powerful man in the Japanese government. Nichiren Shōnin hoped that Tokiyori, as a priest, would understand the reasoning in his essay and use his influence to apply Nichiren Shōnin's remedy for the Japanese people.

Nichiren Shōnin hoped that the government would stop sponsoring what he considered to be heretical Buddhist ceremonies and would start using the teaching of the *Lotus Sutra*. Instead, the government entirely ignored the *Risshō Ankoku Ron*.

While he waited for a response from the government, Nichiren Shōnin returned to his street ministry. As time went by without an official response, however, he began to include his conclusions from his essay in his sermons. This gained new attention for Nichiren Shōnin; now not only simple lay believers in Pure Land Buddhism were angered by his remarks, but priests of many Buddhist schools found him offensive. More dangerously, the government was less than pleased by his criticism of their handling of the disasters.

Persecution and the First Exile

Unfortunately, the government officials who were now paying attention to Nichiren Shōnin were not impressed by his reasoning nor by the scriptures that he quoted. Further, the Pure Land priests were not about to allow their almost unquestioned superiority in religious matters be questioned by one young priest from the provinces. Spurred on by angry Pure Land priests—and possibly by one of Tokiyori Hōjō's relatives in retaliation for the critique of the government—an angry mob torched the hut in which Nichiren Shōnin was living at Matsubagayatsu on August 27, 1260. This incident, known as the Matsubagayatsu Persecution, was the first of many trials that Nichiren Shōnin would undergo. Legend says that Nichiren Shōnin was saved from the fire when a white monkey awoke him before the mob arrived.

Nichiren Shōnin fled back to the outlying provinces, where he had achieved success before with the provincial lords. He again was able to convert some of the people to whom he preached, but Nichiren Shōnin's stay away from the capital was destined to be a short one. He had to return to preach among those with power if the nation was to be endowed with the Buddha's true teaching. Therefore, after only a few months, Nichiren Shōnin returned to Kamakura hoping that tempers has eased during his absence.

Perhaps his opponents' tempers had eased during that time, but it did not take long for them to flare up again. Nichiren Shōnin began preaching again, and his message had not changed. Some powerful Pure Land priests went to the government and insisted that they silence him. The government was not inclined to disagree with the priests, since they also considered Nichiren Shōnin a problem. It was easy for them to come to an agreement without even hearing from Nichiren Shōnin himself. He was to be arrested and exiled to remote Izu Peninsula. This sentence was carried out on May 12, 1261 for the charge of "disturbing the peace."

Itō Village on Izu Peninsula, by today's standards of transportation, looks almost comically close to Kyōto and even Kamakura for a place of exile. However, in Nichiren Shōnin's time, it was a common place to send political exiles. The only reasonably safe way to get to the village of Itō was by boat.

In such a boat, Nichiren Shōnin was taken to his place of exile. However, he was not quite taken to shore: whether from animosity or simply because they wished to return home as soon as possible, the boatmen dropped Nichiren Shōnin on a spar of land that with the rising tide would soon be under water. Fortunately, one of the fishermen of Itō named Yasaburō Funamori saw Nichiren Shōnin from his boat. Yasaburō rowed to the rapidly vanishing rock and saved Nichiren Shōnin from drowning.

Nichiren Shōnin stranded on the rocks off the coast of the Izu Peninsula.

Itō was the one place of civilization on the peninsula, and it was not open to exiles. There was no real shelter, and whatever rough food there was would be difficult to find. Concerned about this, Yasaburō and his wife offered to give Nichiren Shōnin a place in their own home. However, Nichiren Shōnin could not accept the offer. He knew that if they were caught aiding an exile, their own freedom would be at risk. The poor couple insisted on helping him find shelter outside of their house, however, and they could not allow the young priest to starve, no matter how sternly he told them not to give him food. Besides being his benefactors in his time of need, the old couple became his friends as well. After hearing his ideas about Buddhism, they also became Nichiren Shōnin's followers.

They were not to be his only followers in the remote province of Izu, however. The lord of the province, Hachirōzaemon Itō, was very sick when Nichiren Shōnin arrived. His mind was so affected by his illness that he was not aware of what was going on around him. He did not even know that the religious dissident and exile was in his province. Hachirōzaemon's loyal retainers knew, though.

Hachirōzaemon's followers had almost given up hope for their lord. Buddhist priests had prayed for him and doctors had attended on him, but they now all considered him beyond hope. In desperation, the lord's followers sought out Nichiren Shōnin and begged him to pray for Hachirōzaemon. Despite his exile, Nichiren Shōnin was a man of true compassion. He truly wanted to relieve the suffering of all people—this was why he preached the ideas that had gotten him exiled. So Nichiren Shōnin was perfectly willing to pray for the lord of his place of exile. Using the teaching of the *Lotus Sutra*, Nichiren Shōnin prayed for

Hachirōzaemon and instructed his followers in treating the sick lord. Within days, Hachirōzaemon had recovered to the point that his mind was restored. In gratitude, Hachirōzaemon gave the exiled priest a small statue of Śākyamuni Buddha that Nichiren Shōnin always carried with him from that day until his death.

The seemingly miraculous recovery of Hachirōzaemon resulted in a considerable change in Nichiren Shōnin's fortunes on Izu. People listened to him preach, and many were converted. He was able to find real shelter, food, and the materials to allow him to write more letters and essays. Finally, on February 22, 1263, Nichiren Shōnin received a pardon allowing him to return from his exile on Izu Peninsula. His pardon was probably due in part to the intercession of Hachirōzaemon on his behalf, though there is some speculation that Tokiyori Hōjō pardoned him because of the unjust circumstances surrounding his exile.

Continuing Persecutions

Nichiren Shōnin returned to Kamakura and was reunited with his disciples. During the Matsubagayatsu Persecution, many of his disciples had deserted him out of fear for their own safety. During the Izu Exile, however, more had the strength and conviction to remain faithful to his teachings, even despite the fact that they had also suffered some persecution both from the government and from believers in the other schools of Buddhism. On Nichiren Shōnin's return, though, some of them did ask him if he might not consider toning down his preaching for his own safety. He had no intention of doing this, however. He was coming to understand that he was living the *Lotus Sutra* with his body; that is, his life was a reflection of its teachings. The *Lotus Sutra* predicted persecution and exile for those who preached it, and Nichiren Shōnin was being persecuted. Further, he read the stories of the *Lotus Sutra* as examples of how a devoted Buddhist should live his or her life. The *Lotus Sutra* was not simply stories and metaphors for Nichiren Shōnin, it was a model for Buddhist life and a prophecy of what a Buddhist would experience in applying its teachings.

So Nichiren Shōnin continued his preaching against the decadent schools of Buddhism, implored the people to take up faith in the *Lotus Sutra*, and railed against the government's reliance on ineffective Buddhist rituals. His conviction in the truth of his awakening would not be deterred by concerns for his own safety.

Undoubtedly, Nichiren Shōnin would have stayed in Kamakura preaching the truth of the *Lotus Sutra*, but news arrived from his home province: his mother was desperately ill and on the edge of death. The anger and death threat of Kagenobu Tōjō had prevented Nichiren Shōnin from returning to Kominato in the past, even when his father had suddenly died some years previously, but even the danger of execution could not keep him from his mother's deathbed. Nichiren Shōnin hurried to his home town.

His mother was desperately ill. When Nichiren Shōnin arrived, she was thought to be beyond all help. Nichiren Shōnin recited portions of the *Lotus Sutra* by her bed to ease her passing and chanted the Odaimoku. As he chanted, she started regaining consciousness. Miraculously, she began recovering. She would live for another four years.

Having seen his mother and knowing that she was out of danger, Nichiren Shōnin went to visit his old master, Dōzen-bo, at Seichōji on November 11, 1264. He also had an invitation from one of the lords who had converted to his teaching, Yoshitaka Kudō, to visit his estate. Nichiren Shōnin's visit with Dōzen-bo was disappointing; his teacher, though sympathetic to his former student, was unable to bring himself to convert from his faith in Pure Land Buddhism. Somewhat disheartened, Nichiren Shōnin left the temple and started on his way to Kudō's estate.

It was a short journey that took the priest and his small group of followers through the forest of Komatsubara, laying on the edge of Kagenobu Tōjō's estate. As the group entered the forest, a group of over one hundred men attacked them. Lord Tōjō had heard of Nichiren Shōnin's return and somehow had discovered the priest's travel plans for that night.

The fight was very uneven. Several priests and a couple of samurai were arrayed against the full strength of a lord. However, in the dark and with the trees as shelter, the small group was not annihilated. The sounds of battle also drew Lord Kudō and a small band of retainers to Nichiren Shōnin's aid. However, both Lord Kudō and another member of Nichiren Shōnin's group were mortally wounded in the fight, and two more received serious injuries. Lord Tōjō himself came after Nichiren Shōnin with his sword and very nearly beheaded him. But the priest's prayer beads frightened Lord Tōjō's horse, causing the deadly blow to glance off of Nichiren Shōnin's head, only inflicting a minor cut. Lord Tōjō himself was thrown from his horse and knocked senseless. In the resulting confusion, Nichiren Shōnin and his surviving followers were able to escape.

Nichiren Shōnin saw this deadly attack as evidence that the Pure Land Buddhists were still a major threat to him. More than that, he was shaken by the fact that several of his followers had been injured and killed by his enemies. He decided once again to allow his adversaries to cool off, and to strengthen his support among the people. He returned

to the outlying provinces, converting more rural lords and many of the
common people. He remained in the outer provinces for four years;
then, in 1268, current events called him back to Kamakura.

An envoy from China had arrived with a message. The Mongolian
invaders of Kublai Khan, who had conquered all of mainland China,
had sent the government of Japan an ultimatum: either accept the
Mongolians as overlords and pay tribute, or suffer invasion and total
overthrow.

To Nichiren Shōnin, this was fulfillment of his prophecy. In *Risshō
Ankoku Ron*, he had warned that if Japan continued to support the false
schools of Buddhism, it would face invasion by foreign forces. The protective heavenly deities (the *kami*) would no longer protect the country
while the government slandered the teaching of Śākyamuni Buddha
found in the *Lotus Sutra*.

Because his predictions were coming true, Nichiren Shōnin returned
to Kamakura to remind the government of his warnings, and to urge
them once again to apply the remedy that he had prescribed. Not only
did he return to his fiery street preaching, he also sent messages to the
military government, imploring them to heed his words in his essay.
These messages, like his original essay, were ignored.

The Mongols sent several more envoys to Japan. They, like Nichiren
Shōnin's messages, were ignored—or rebuked—by the government. By
1271, no more messages were coming from the Mongols, and the government believed the danger had passed.

However, another problem arose to unsettle the people: a drought.
For months that summer, no rain fell; the crops and the food supply
were in serious danger. The government called on Ryōkan, a leading
Pure Land priest, to pray for rain. When Nichiren Shōnin heard of
Ryōkan's acceptance, he was more concerned than ever. Nichiren
Shōnin sent the Pure Land priest a challenge: if the Pure Land prayers
brought rain within a week, Nichiren Shōnin would convert and
become his disciple; but if they did not work, Ryōkan would convert to
Nichiren Shōnin's teaching. Ryōkan was sure of that his prayers would
work, and believed he would be able to quiet Nichiren Shōnin's criti-
cisms. However, despite seven days of high Pure Land ritual, no rain
fell.

Ryōkan had no intention of becoming Nichiren Shōnin's follower.
Instead, the priest met with Hei-no Yoritsuna, a high government official who was also a Pure Land Buddhist. Together, they brought a
charge of treason against Nichiren Shōnin to the government, claiming
that he sought to undermine Buddhism and the government. The government leaders believed the charge and put Yoritsuna, the very man
who had written the indictment, in charge of the investigation.

Execution, Sado, and the Object of Devotion

Needless to say, Nichiren Shōnin was found guilty. Yoritsuna's troops surrounded Nichiren Shōnin's home at Matsubagayatsu and attacked the priest as he was talking to his disciples. He was seized, and one of Yoritsuna's men grabbed a scroll of the *Lotus Sutra* from Nichiren Shōnin and beat him on the head with it.

This incident was very important to Nichiren Shōnin. It confirmed that he was fulfilling the prophecies of the *Lotus Sutra* with his own body, because the very scroll with which he was beaten, the fifth, contains the passage that says that those who follow the *Lotus Sutra* will be beaten with sticks. Nichiren Shōnin later wrote about the incident, "I have already been hit in the face by Shoubō with the fifth scroll of the *Lotus Sutra*. The exact scroll he used as a stick to beat me says that the keeper of the sutra will be attacked with sticks. What a miracle that Shoubō proved the prediction of the sutra!"

Yoritsuna's men brought Nichiren Shōnin before the court of the government, where the verdict was a foregone conclusion: guilty, with a sentence of banishment on Sado Island. Nichiren Shōnin was given into Yoritsuna's custody to await his deportation. Yoritsuna, however, did not plan to allow the priest to live, so he ordered that Nichiren Shōnin be executed immediately.

That afternoon, September 12, 1271, Nichiren Shōnin was tied to a horse and paraded through the streets of the capital, a fate usually reserved for common criminals. During this parade, the group passed the shrine to Hachiman, the Buddhist patron deity of Japan. As they reached the shrine, Nichiren Shōnin requested to be allowed to stop and speak to the great bodhisattva. His guards and many of the people believed that he would humbly beg for forgiveness or intercession from Hachiman. Instead, he began to admonish the god. All of the Buddhist gods had promised to protect the keeper of the *Lotus Sutra* when Śākyamuni preached it; where was he now when Nichiren Shōnin was being taken to his death? Unless Hachiman and the Sun Goddess wanted to be known as liars before the Buddha and the people of Japan, they had better get busy protecting the *Lotus Sutra*'s followers! As he finished his rebuke of the Buddhist deities and saints and the procession resumed, many of the people began to wonder if he was insane. Others began to think that his unrelenting certainty showed that he was himself a saint.

As the group continued on its way to the execution ground at Tatsunokuchi Beach, some of Nichiren Shōnin's followers began to join the group including one of his best-known lay-disciples, the samurai Kingo Shijō. All were heartbroken and in tears, but Nichiren Shōnin quieted them, reminding them that there was no greater joy for him than to die in the cause of the Buddha Dharma.

Finally, shortly after midnight, the group—Nichiren Shōnin, his devoted followers, and the guards—arrived at Tatsunokuchi Beach. Yoritsuna sat as official witness, and the executioner awaited with his sword. As Nichiren Shōnin knelt within the circle of guards, his followers gasped with dread and anticipation. Nichiren Shōnin remained calm, however, pressed his hands together in reverence, and chanted "Namu Myōhō Renge Kyō." He then bent his head, exposing his neck for the executioner's sword.

All were certain that these would be the last words of Nichiren Shōnin, one of the few Buddhist priests to be executed as a common criminal in the history of Japan to that point. However, it was not to be. A vast ball of light shot across the sky, so bright that it illuminated the crowd on the beach, as bright or even brighter than the full moon. Terrified, the executioner fell to the ground, his sword shattering into pieces. Many of the guards fled, others prostrated themselves on the ground. Even the haughty Yoritsuna fled.

The remaining officials decided that the priest should be kept in safety until further council could be taken regarding his fate. He was taken in the early morning light to the estate of a nearby lord, where he was greeted and held with some deference.

In the meantime, a debate was occurring within the government. Some officials were displeased with the way Nichiren Shōnin was being treated. They were able to convince the leader of the military government, Tokimune, that no purpose would be served by executing a Buddhist priest. Tokimune, who was somewhat ambivalent about Nichiren Shōnin, finally agreed: he must be banished to Sado, but he must not be killed. Word of his reprieve arrived at the estate where he was being held the evening of the day after he had arrived there.

The attempted execution had a profound effect on Nichiren Shōnin. Writing later, Nichiren said, "Tatsunokuchi is the place where Nichiren renounced his life." He now felt that he was living the prophecies of the *Lotus Sutra* in their entirety. No longer was Nichiren Shōnin simply attempting to reform Buddhism; the attempted execution and the intervention of the protective forces of Buddhism had revealed Nichiren Shōnin's identity as the propagator of the *Lotus Sutra* in the Declining Age of the Dharma. From that point forward, he would refer to himself as the person who was doing the work of Bodhisattva Superb Action, the leader of the Bodhisattvas of the Earth from Chapter Fifteen of the *Lotus Sutra* (see Chapter 7 of this book).

Nichiren Shōnin was taken by boat to Sado Island and arrived there on October 28, 1271. Incredibly remote, wind-blown, and subject to severe winters, this was the most severe place of exile in Japan. But even this was not harsh enough for the government; they may have finally been unwilling—or unable—to execute Nichiren Shōnin, but he was to be punished most severely. His captors took him to an abandoned graveyard shrine at Tsukahara and decreed that this dilapidated and defiled hut would be his home in exile—for the rest of his life, however short that would be in these extreme conditions.

Abandoned in a place which did not even offer shelter from the elements, life did seem particularly grim, if not almost unsurvivable, to Nichiren Shōnin and the few disciples that had been able to follow him into exile. But even greater danger than the weather awaited Nichiren Shōnin. An old samurai named Abutsu had been living on Sado since he had followed the former Emperor Juntoku into exile on the island. Abutsu was a pious believer in Pure Land Buddhism, so devout that he had become a lay minister after the death of his exiled master. He had heard of the arrival of the exiled enemy of his faith on the island and had determined that he himself would kill the heretical priest.

Abutsu was a man of strict honor, however, so when he arrived at Tsukahara to kill Nichiren Shōnin, he first allowed the priest to speak on his own behalf. By the time the conversation was over, Abutsu's thoughts of killing Nichiren Shōnin were gone; the old samurai had been convinced to convert. Abutsu and his wife provided Nichiren Shōnin and his small group with the supplies necessary for survival for the remainder of that winter.

Throughout his first winter more curious local people came to see Nichiren Shōnin and many were converted, including some Pure Land priests. Also during that winter his young disciple Nichirō secretly came to visit.

Nichirō had himself been imprisoned at the time of Tatsunokuchi with another young priest, Nisshin. While in prison, they had so earnestly prayed for their master's safety that their guard, moved by their devotion, had secretly allowed Nichirō to go free to visit Nichiren Shōnin.

Nichirō somehow managed to make the journey across Japan and onto Sado Island. However, when Nichiren Shōnin saw the young priest he was quite angry. His priestly disciples had never broken the law before—this could give justification to those who used the courts in an attempt to quiet Nichiren Shōnin. Furthermore, Nichirō was endangering the safety of the prison guard who let him free. Nichirō saw the error of his actions and made ready to return. Nichiren Shōnin then encouraged his devout disciple, assuring him that they would meet again when his exile ended—as Nichiren Shōnin was sure it would when more of his predictions came true.

As the spring of 1272 ripened, Pure Land and other Buddhist priests from the mainland, who had been hearing with increasing alarm the stories of Nichiren Shōnin's success at conversion, decided that they would hold a debate with him. Surely with enough scholarly priests speaking against him, the renegade could be silenced and those led astray by him could be convinced to recant. But these arrogant priests were, like so many before them, unable to prevail against Nichiren Shōnin. In fact, many of those who had come hoping to silence him were themselves converted to Nichiren Shōnin's truth.

At about this time, another of Nichiren Shōnin's predictions was fulfilled. There was a violent tremor within the ruling Hōjō clan, almost to the point of a palace coup. Tokimune was forced to have his own brother killed to maintain stability within the government. Tokimune remembered Nichiren Shōnin's prediction that there would be strife within the ruling family. Though by no means reconciled with the fiery priest, he was impressed enough to send orders to Sado that Nichiren Shōnin be protected and cared for in exile. Most immediately, this resulted in Nichiren Shōnin being given proper shelter at Ichinosawa.

The easing of the terms of his banishment allowed Nichiren Shōnin to begin work on some of the most important tasks he had before him. Principle among these was the production of a focus of devotion, the Most Venerable One, for those who believed in the *Lotus Sutra*. In preparation, he would write two of his most important essays.

The first of these works was the essay known as *Open Your Eyes to the Lotus Teaching* (*Kaimoku Shō*). In it, Nichiren Shōnin laid out an ethical structure for his followers. The teachings which had come before Buddhism, Confucianism and Brahmanism, provided a basic moral framework for society. Hinayana Buddhism had introduced the beginning of Buddhist philosophy. Pre-*Lotus Sutra* Mahāyāna Buddhism had introduced the selfless ethics of the bodhisattva. However, though Nichiren Shōnin's ethics were based on these systems, *Open Your Eyes to the Lotus Teaching* also provided a means of comparison between all of the systems. Each of the previous teachings showed only a portion of the truth; they were incomplete in themselves. Only the *Lotus Sutra* is complete; we can find ethical truths in other systems only when they are viewed through the lens of the *Lotus Sutra*.

Nichiren Shōnin next wrote an essay to describe the exact form of the Most Venerable One and explain the reasons for its form. This work was called *Treatise on Revealing Spiritual Contemplation and the Most Venerable One* (*Kanjin Honzon Shō*). In it, the requirements for the focus of devotion for meditation are laid out so that there can be no confusion between the valid object, the Eternal Śākyamuni Buddha revealed in the *Lotus Sutra*, and provisional, invalid objects.

Once the doctrinal groundwork had been laid, Nichiren Shōnin was ready to create an actual depiction of the Most Venerable One for those who followed his teachings. On July 8, 1273, he inscribed a Most Venerable One (*Gohonzon*) in the form of a calligraphic Great Mandala. In flowing script Chinese characters—with two Sanskrit characters to represent two "universal forces"—Nichiren Shōnin created a diagram of the great gathering described in the core of the *Lotus Sutra*, the Assembly in the Air. Because it contains beings from every state of existence, this ceremony also encapsulates the teaching that all beings can become Buddhas because they all contain the nature of the Buddha within themselves. The Odaimoku runs down the center of the Gohonzon, indicating that through reciting the Odaimoku we can plant the seed of Buddhahood and access our Buddha nature. See Chapter 2 for more information about the Most Venerable One and the doctrines that it represents.

Final Return to Kamakura and Retirement to Minobu

Even as Nichiren Shōnin wrote these scholarly works and created the mandala depiction of the Most Venerable One, he continued to speak to the people and win converts. Even a member of the ruling clan, Tokimori Hōjō (also known as Yagenta), had converted to his teachings.

Just as Nichiren Shōnin continued working on developing Buddhism, the events of history were also moving forward. Besides the strife within the government, the Mongols had resumed sending envoys to Japan, this time with very specific threats: Pay tribute or be invaded. Toward the end of 1273, it became quite clear that the Mongolian hordes were preparing to invade in the very near future.

The regent Tokimune was desperate. Probably with some prodding from his clan member Tokimori, Tokimune recalled the prophecies and teachings of Nichiren Shōnin. In February of 1274, he officially ended the priest's exile and called him to Kamakura for advice on averting the Mongol invasion.

Nichiren Shōnin's followers had for some time been lobbying for his release. However, Nichiren Shōnin had always asked them to stop their efforts, because he did not think that the government was ready to listen to him. Now, though, the government itself seemed to be favoring his teachings. He prepared to leave, made heartfelt farewells to all of the friends and converts he had made during his exile, especially Abutsu, and departed for the capital.

It was good that Tokimune had provided a government escort for the priest. Infuriated by the sudden rise of Nichiren Shōnin, their most inimical foe—an occurrence as unexpected as a blizzard in the hottest days of summer—various Pure Land priests attempted to ambush and kill him several times during his journey back to Kamakura. Because of the protection of the guards, they were unsuccessful and Nichiren

Shōnin arrived at the capital on March 26, 1274, to prepare for a meeting with the military leaders of the government.

On April 8, Nichiren Shōnin was called to the palace for his consultation. Ironically, the person who had to provide him with hospitality and politely beg spiritual advice from him was Hei-no Yoritsuna, the implacable enemy of Nichiren Shōnin who had tried to behead him only three years before. Nichiren Shōnin, ignoring whatever hypocrisy or discomfort Hei-no Yoritsuna may have felt, stated again his prescription for saving Japan: withdraw support from the outmoded schools of Buddhism and uphold the Eternal Śākyamuni Buddha and the *Lotus Sutra*.

Much to the government's surprise, the years of exile had not bent Nichiren Shōnin's resolve. They were faced with a politically impossible choice: to either comply with Nichiren Shōnin's demands and shut down all of the other Buddhist sects, or to ignore the advice of the person that they had called back from exile. The second choice was difficult because in pardoning Nichiren Shōnin the government had essentially admitted that they had made a mistake in their original judgment. In that society at that time, this could cause a major loss in public standing; ignoring the advice that they had risked their standing to get would almost certainly have caused a fall in their prestige. Furthermore, they wanted to stifle Nichiren Shōnin's criticism of them—and, just in case he was right, get him to offer prayers for them to defeat the Mongols.

Finally, the government settled on a compromise. They offered Nichiren Shōnin an enormous donation, leadership of a major temple with high nationally-recognized clerical rank, and ongoing public funding for his missionary work and teaching. Nichiren Shōnin did not fall for this ploy; he saw that they had not offered to withdraw support for the other Buddhist schools and felt that their alleged reliance on the *Lotus Sutra* was only lip-service. He did not accept their offer and repeated his admonitions. He warned them that if they did not uphold the *Lotus Sutra*, the country would be invaded by the Mongols before the end of the year.

Soon enough, his suspicions about the government's sincerity was proved. Another drought had struck Japan. Within weeks of their offer to Nichiren Shōnin, the government funded esoteric Buddhist rituals for rain. At first, everyone believed that the rituals had been effective, for it did indeed rain. However, the rain brought with it a typhoon which flooded fields, killed people, and even severely damaged the imperial palace, an omen of dreadful meaning. However, not even this seemed to convince the government of the truth of Nichiren Shōnin's words.

Nichiren Shōnin himself could see that the government leaders did not have the courage to give up their long-held beliefs, no matter how much they were warned nor how much misfortune came to them. There is a Chinese proverb that a sage who has warned his lord three times of his errors and is still not heeded should retire to the mountains. Nichiren Shōnin took this advice, leaving the capital city for Mount Minobu on May 12, 1274.

Mount Minobu at that time was wild country. Surrounded by mountains and covered with forest, the hut that was Nichiren Shōnin's retreat was largely cut off from the surrounding world. However, even in this remote location, he continued to communicate with his followers, and there were now quite a few. As he sent them letters of thanks, encouragement, and guidance, they sent him offerings to show their sincere gratitude.

In the outside world, Nichiren Shōnin's predictions about the country again came true. In the fall of that year, just as he had predicted in his meetings with the government, the Mongols did indeed invade Japan. Their first attack was on the western islands; these territories fell quickly to the enormous armies of Kublai Khan. Many died, and complete invasion seemed very close. But a typhoon came and destroyed most of the Mongol fleet, whereupon the few survivors fled back to the mainland. Unsurprisingly, the esoteric and Pure Land Buddhists took credit for the "victory," though the simple fact was that the Mongolians had not yet learned that typhoons came at a certain time of year—the season that they favored for invasions. Nichiren Shōnin himself was unimpressed by the supposed victory, and predicted future problems with the Mongols. In fact, within a year Kublai Khan sent another envoy with a new threat. This time, the military government executed the envoy and sent his head back to Kublai Khan; with such an insult, further hostilities were inevitable.

But Nichiren Shōnin had other things to do besides lamenting the foolishness of the Japanese government. He had to complete the doctrinal foundation of his school of Buddhism—now a new school, since he realized that the Tendai school would never return to its original teachings, much less follow the *Lotus Sutra*'s instructions regarding the cur-

Nichiren Shōnin studying.

rent time. In 1275, he wrote *Treatise on Selecting the Time* (*Senji shō*), which established the doctrinal basis showing that the time had come to uphold the teaching of the *Lotus Sutra* exclusively. This essay also gave the doctrinal background for the practices of the *Lotus Sutra* that

Nichiren Shōnin had discovered within the *Lotus Sutra*. Finally, he laid the groundwork for the Three Great Hidden Dharmas (see Chapter 2 for details) that are the basis of Nichiren Shōnin's school.

In July 1276, Nichiren Shōnin heard that his oldest teacher, Dōzen-bo, had died at Seichōji. Dōzen-bo had never been able to find the will power to convert to Nichiren Shōnin's teachings, but towards the end of his life he had tentatively begun to worship Śākyamuni Buddha instead of the Buddha of the Pure Land. In response to Dōzen-bo's death, he wrote the last of his five most important essays, the *Treatise on Gratitude* (*Hōon jō*). In this work, he emphasized the debt he felt to his parents and his teacher. However, he emphasized the fact that one did not repay that debt by following these people blindly, but if they were in error, the debt is repaid more properly by working to teach them the truth even if it is against their wishes. Also, Nichiren Shōnin firmed up the doctrine of the Three Great Hidden Dharmas and built a substantial case against the erroneous teachings of esoteric forms of Buddhism.

Yet, even as Nichiren Shōnin firmed the foundations of his teaching, the persecution of those who had faith in it was renewed. Since the claims of esoteric and Pure Land Buddhists to have saved the country from the Mongols, the government seemed to have forgotten the respect they had offered to Nichiren Shōnin after his return from exile. His followers were therefore at risk of being arrested as heretics. And so it came to pass—between 1277 and 1281 many of his followers were arrested, several were executed, and some were subjected to persecution from prejudiced civilians.

This brought much grief to Nichiren Shōnin, who wrote letters of encouragement to afflicted followers and mentioned his concerns in letters to others. However, the reaction of his lay believers to these persecutions gave him hope. In the past, all too often when times got tough, many of his lay followers would renounce their faith. Now Nichiren Shōnin saw evidence of growing resolve and deepening faith; his followers were remaining firm in the face of persecution. These steadfast followers would carry on faith in the *Lotus Sutra* and the Eternal Buddha when he had passed on.

In 1281, the government and the followers of the wayward schools of Buddhism once again became too busy to torment Nichiren Shōnin and his followers. Inevitably, the Mongol horde had chosen to invade Japan again. However, Kublai Khan still had not divined the seasonal pattern of the typhoons and the invasion fleet was once again destroyed. As they did the previous time, the esoteric Buddhists claimed that the victory was theirs.

Nichiren Shōnin saw it differently: If there was a victory, then why did the government not have Kublai Khan captive? The wind had blown the Mongol forces away, as it undoubtedly would have done without either the government or esoteric rituals. Esoteric Buddhism,

Dates in Nichiren Shōnin's Life
Birth
February 16, 1222
Proclamation of Odaimoku
April 28, 1253
Submission of *Risshō Ankoku Ron*
July 16, 1260
Matsubagayatsu Persecution
August 27, 1260
Izu Exile
May 12, 1261
Komatsubara Persecution
November 11, 1264
Tatsunokuchi Persecution
September 12, 1271
Sado Exile
October 10, 1271
Inscription of First Great Mandala
July 8, 1273
Pardon from Sado Exile
February 1274
Retirement to Mount Minobu
May 12, 1274
Death
October 13, 1282

said Nichiren Shōnin, as he had said before, would ruin the nation.

History was to prove Nichiren Shōnin right, though neither he nor most of the other players in this drama lived to see it. Based on the success of "their" typhoons—which, strangely enough, had been manifesting every year long before their school had been founded—the esoteric Buddhist priests convinced the Hōjō regents to spend enormous sums of money on them and on lavish esoteric rituals. This led to bankruptcy, inability to pay the warriors who actually protected them, and, within less than 100 years, the collapse of the Hōjō government. The result was centuries of social strife and virtual anarchy.

Nichiren Shōnin's Death

In spite of the continued accuracy of his predictions and his unwavering spiritual vigor, years of persecution, wandering, and exile were beginning to take their toll on Nichiren Shōnin's physical health. As early as 1279, he was beginning to show signs of illness. Due to the treatment of his devout disciple Kingo Shijō, doctor as well as samurai, he was able to recover much of his health for several more years.

Though his health was never really complete again, Nichiren Shōnin continued to teach and encourage his followers, both by letter and in person for those who came to see him at Mount Minobu. In late 1281, the local lord with the help of some of Nichiren Shōnin's other wealthy followers constructed a temple hall to accommodate the increased number of pilgrims who were coming to hear the lectures of the master.

But his physical health was failing once more. By the end of the summer of 1282, Nichiren Shōnin could not hide his suffering any more. On

September 8, he set out from Mount Minobu for the first time since he had arrived there. He planned to make his way to a hot spring northeast of Tokyo in Hitachi to either effect a cure or at least ease his pain. However, when on September 18th he arrived at the house of one of his followers, Lord Munenaka Ikegami, in present-day Tokyo, he found he could travel no further.

Knowing that the end was near, Nichiren Shōnin wrote to his devoted follower, Lord Hakii, to thank him for the support and protection he had extended throughout Nichiren Shōnin's many difficulties. Near the end, Nichiren Shōnin instructed Lord Hakii as to where he wanted his tomb to be made: "Make a tomb for me at Minobu wherever I may pass away." (*Hakii dono gosho*, Christensen, page 121)

Yet Nichiren Shōnin continued to receive his followers, to give them advice and encouragement. But by October 13th, the end was at hand. Surrounded by his followers, the great priest of the *Lotus Sutra* died chanting its words.

Chapter 5
Nichiren Shonin's Writings

An important inspiration to all followers of Nichiren Buddhism are the writings of the Nichiren Shōnin himself. Despite his dramatic life, filled with persecution and turmoil, Nichiren Shōnin was able to compose a great number of essays and letters. Not only do these writings, called Go-ibun or Gosho in Japanese, detail his philosophies and doctrines, they also often reveal a warm man concerned about the well-being of his followers and of all living beings. His writings are therefore spiritually uplifting to Nichiren Buddhists. They have also served to clarify the thinking of Nichiren Shōnin when disputes as to doctrine have occurred in the time since he passed away.

Classifications of Nichiren Shōnin's Writings

There are several ways to classify Nichiren Shōnin's writings. They can be categorized according to the time during which he wrote them, by their contents, by subject, and by their authenticity. We will look at classification by content and authenticity, as the other two classifications exceed the scope of this book.

By Content

Nichiren Shōnin left five basic kinds of writing:

1. Technical essays such as *Open Your Eyes to the Lotus Teaching*. These writings are clear explanations of Nichiren Shōnin's doctrines and philosophies, obviously written to explain his thoughts to his followers and to others. They are typically written in classical Chinese, the language of educated Japanese people in his time.

2. Letters sent to specific followers and disciples. The most numerous of his writings, these works reveal Nichiren Shōnin's deep compassion and affection for his followers, as well as his gratitude for their offerings. These works often answer a follower's specific questions, or offer him or her encouragement and guidance. Some are congratulations or condolences for events in the person's life. Many explain doctrinal issues or questions of Buddhist practice, always at the level of the recipient's understanding. These are written either in classical Chinese or in the common, colloquial Japanese writing, depending on the level of education of the person to whom the letter is addressed.

3. A number of diagrams and charts, graphically representing Nichiren Shōnin's understanding of certain Buddhist concepts.

4. Hand-made copies of other Buddhist writings. Before the invention of printing and copy machines, the only way someone could get a copy was to have it made by hand. Often these copies were made by the person him- or herself, as copyists were expensive. Nichiren Shōnin made many copies of important works for himself. However, very few of these contain any of Nichiren Shōnin's own thoughts.

5. Great Mandalas. A Great Mandala represents the Most Venerable One. Nichiren Shōnin created this graphic representation of the Eternal Buddha performing the Transmission of the Dharma for his followers' use. One-hundred twenty-five of these still survive.

Today, 493 essays and letters, 365 fragments of letters, 125 Great Mandalas, 36 diagrams, and 163 copied texts still survive.

By Authenticity

Understandably, there have been times since Nichiren Shōnin's death when disagreements have arisen within the Nichiren Buddhist community as to the meaning of some doctrines. Of course, the simplest answer to any disagreement would be finding out exactly what Nichiren Shōnin said about the point in question. Unfortunately, this is not always as easy as it sounds.

There are certainly some alleged Nichiren Shōnin writings that are not authentic. These were introduced for various reasons, such as sincere desire to expand the understanding of Buddhism and, unfortunately, occasionally to provide "proof" for one's own side in a disagreement. Because Nichiren Shōnin's writings are used to evaluate the truth of doctrine and understanding, it is important to separate his authentic work from false works. Some of the questionable works can be very inspiring, and can certainly be used to lift our spirits, but they should be approached with caution when dealing with doctrinal understanding.

Of the 493 complete essays and letters, 308 can be considered positively to be the work of Nichiren Shōnin by the strictest scholars. These either exist in Nichiren Shōnin's own handwriting, those that exist in the handwriting of Nichiren Shōnin's direct disciples and are marked as being copies from a Nichiren Shōnin original by that disciple, and those that are historically known to have existed in Nichiren Shōnin's handwriting before being lost (such as those destroyed in a fire at Kuon-ji temple in 1875). The most reliable source for Nichiren Shōnin's doctrines, however, are his five major writings, listed in the summary below. Some of Nichiren Shōnin's letters to followers of simple faith and education explain doctrines from a limited perspective, accessible to the intended recipient; those perspectives are broadened in his doctrinal essays and letters to more educated followers, so again one must be careful not to extract dogmatic ideas from single quotes within his letters. Statements in the major essays, when read in context, can be relied on for doctrinal understanding.

Because of the age of the texts, questions occasionally arise regarding the accuracy of the reading of some texts. The standard source considered reliable both by Nichiren Shu and by most scholars is the *Shōwa Teihon Nichiren Shōnin Ibun*. This collection indicates any possible alternate readings of the original texts. The *Shōwa Teihon* also divides the writings into those that are indisputably authentic and those that are of questionable origin. These facts make the work the most important source for serious students of Japanese Buddhism.

Summary of Nichiren Shōnin's Most Important Writings

The Five Major Writings

Treatise on Spreading Peace Throughout the Country by Establishing the True Dharma
(*Risshō Ankoku-ron*)

This is the best known of all of Nichiren Shōnin's writings. It was written in 1260 when Nichiren Shōnin was thirty-nine. This essay displays the foundation of Nichiren Shōnin's thought and is the text which launched him into prominence. Because of this, it is included among his five most important works.

At the time Nichiren Shōnin wrote this essay, Japan had been suffering from a series of earthquakes, famines, epidemics, and strange events in the heavens. The whole nation was suffering social unrest, and everyone was afraid and depressed. Searching for the cause of these unprecedented troubles, Nichiren Shōnin read through the entire Buddhist canon. He found that the sutras did contain teachings that applied to the situation of Japan at that time. They said that unless people stopped practicing forms of Buddhism that were in error and began to trust solely in the true Dharma of the *Lotus Sutra*, Japan would probably experience domestic rebellion and foreign invasion in the near future. The form of Buddhism that he particularly criticized was the Pure Land doctrines. Nichiren Shōnin concluded the essay by stating that if Japan were to rely exclusively on the *Lotus Sutra*, this world would become the purified land of the Buddha. Because of the implied criticism of the government in this work, however, when Nichiren Shōnin presented it to the leaders of Japan, the government became hostile towards him and his teachings. That hostility would follow him for the rest of his life.

This text survives in its original manuscript.

Open Your Eyes to the Lotus Teaching
(*Kaimoku-shō*)

This essay was completed in February, 1272, at Tsukahara on Sado Island. It was written at a time of crisis in Nichiren Shōnin's life. He had recently narrowly escaped death both from an attempted execution and the perils of his first winter in exile (see Chapter 4 for the story of Nichiren Shōnin's life). He could not be certain that the recent attempt to execute him would not be repeated, or even that he would live through the dire circumstances of his exile. His followers, both priests and laypeople, were being persecuted wherever they lived. It seemed that everything he had worked for was on the brink of destruction. Feeling that he did not have long to live, Nichiren Shōnin wrote that the composition of this treatise was probably "the last great event of my life."

Nevertheless, in this essay he declares his conviction that he is the leader of humanity in the Declining Age of the Dharma. For this reason, *Open Your Eyes to the Lotus Teaching* is also referred to as "Revelation of the Man," and ranks with the *Treatise on Revealing Spiritual Contemplation and the Most Venerable One* (see below), which is known as the "Revelation of the Teaching," as the heart of Nichiren Shōnin's doctrinal works. However, before he reveals himself as the leader of people in the Declining Age of the Dharma, he establishes the principle of Three Thousand Conditions in One Moment of Thought (ichinen sanzen, see Chapter 2 for a complete explanation) as the basic doctrine for this age. Finally, he asks who is doing the work of Bodhisattva Superb Action, who was given the mission of spreading the *Lotus Sutra* by Śākyamuni Buddha during the Declining Age of the Dharma. Demonstrating that his determined efforts to spread the *Lotus Sutra* matched the descriptions in the sutra itself, he proclaims that he is the leader who was forecast for this age. He vows, "I will be the pillar, the eyes, and the great vessel of Japan."

In this essay, Nichiren Shōnin explains that the suffering we experience for propagating the *Lotus Sutra* is our way of expiating our karma for having slandered the Dharma in the past. He also shows that *shakubuku*—that is, breaking people of their false beliefs by direct statements—is the correct method of ministry in the Declining Age of the Dharma. With its general summary of Nichiren Shōnin's doctrinal tenets and its emphasis on the experiences that paved the way for his ministry, *Open Your Eyes to the Lotus Teaching* is the clearest presentation of Nichiren Shōnin's thought and faith among all of his works.

Though the text of this essay is certainly authentic, the original manuscript was lost in a fire in 1875.

Treatise on Revealing Spiritual Contemplation and the Most Venerable One
(*Kanjin Honzon-shō*)

The full title of this work is *A Treatise Revealing the Spiritual Insight and the Most Venerable One for the First Time in the Fifth 500-year Period After the Death of Śākyamuni Buddha* (*Nyorai metsugo go-gohyaku-sai-shi kanjin honzon-shō*). The lengthy title is usually abbreviated as above. Compiled in April, 1273, on Sado Island, Nichiren Shōnin himself called it "the principal work of my life," as its topic is the ultimate

Dharma which brings salvation in the Declining Age of the Dharma. As
the "Revelation of the Teaching," this text stands with *Opening the Eyes*
at the heart of Nichiren doctrinal studies.

Nichiren Shōnin begins by discussing the meaning of the theoretical
aspects of Three Thousand Conditions in One Moment of Thought
(ichinen sanzen, for which see Chapter 2) first revealed by T'ien T'ai,
and then reveals his realization of the applied (or practical) nature of
this teaching (*ji-no-ichinen sanzen*). According to Nichiren Shōnin, this is
the essential doctrine of the Odaimoku, Namu Myōhō Renge Kyō.
Because of ichinen sanzen, both the Buddha's practice—the cause—and
his enlightenment—the result—are contained naturally within the
Odaimoku. Nichiren Shōnin goes on to discuss the essential substance
and outward appearance of the Most Venerable One (*honzon*) which
reveals the essential doctrine of the Buddha. He explains that by believing in and by chanting the Odaimoku, people in the Declining Age of
the Dharma can unite with the Buddha and cause the eternal Buddha-
land to appear around them in this world. In short, he affirms that the
fundamental Dharma for the Declining Age of the Dharma is the
Odaimoku itself and that the proper leader for the ministry of the *Lotus
Sutra* is the leader of the Bodhisattvas from Underground (see the summary of the *Lotus Sutra* in Chapter 7), whose work is now being done
by Nichiren Shōnin. Three months after writing this essay, on July 8,
1273, Nichiren Shōnin inscribed the first Great Mandala in accordance
with the teaching of this text, the first physical portrayal of the Most
Venerable One.

The original manuscript of this text still survives.

Treatise on Selecting the Time
(*Senji-shō*)

Nichiren Shōnin wrote this essay in June, 1275, eight months after
the first Mongol attack on Japan. In it, he remarks that the prediction
that Japan would be invaded he made in his *Treatise on Spreading Peace
Throughout the Nation by Establishing Righteousness* had come true. In the
earlier essay, he had said that only by trusting solely in the *Lotus Sutra*
could the nation escape the threat of devastation. In *Treatise on Selecting
the Time*, he goes further and says that he himself is the only person
qualified to save the people in this age since he alone possesses the
virtues of a master, teacher, and parent. In other words, this text takes
the principle of teaching appropriate to the time, discusses how this
corresponds to Nichiren Shōnin's method of classifying the Buddhist
scriptures, and establishes his position in Buddhist history as the single
person qualified to be spiritual leader in the Declining Age of the
Dharma. He bases this on the history of the transmission of Buddhism
from the death of the Buddha to the beginning of the Declining Age of

the Dharma, both from the perspective of the Buddha's predictions and actual historical events. The text goes on to strongly reject all the other branches of Buddhism as dangerously flawed, especially the esoteric teachings of Shingon that had also corrupted Tendai Buddhism. Nichiren Shōnin warns that the state's support of these teachings would destroy the country.

Treatise on Gratitude

(*Hōon-jō*)

Nichiren Shōnin wrote the *Treatise on Gratitude* in July, 1276, in memory of his teacher Dōzen-bo, who had recently died. It was carried by Nichiren Shōnin's disciple Nikō to be read at Dōzen-bō's grave at Seichōji. This essay explains that showing gratitude correctly is an important moral responsibility. The text compares the Buddhist sense of gratitude with that of normal worldly ethics. True gratitude is expressed by doing what is right, even if the person to whom you are expressing your gratitude disagrees because of his or her misunderstanding. In Nichiren Buddhism, true gratitude is expressed by propagating the Odaimoku, the essence of the *Lotus Sutra*. The essay traces the history of Buddhism in India, China, and Japan while refuting the mistaken teachings of other schools, especially the esoteric practices of Tendai and Shingon. It also includes a review of the trials suffered by Nichiren Shōnin. One of the most important teachings in the *Treatise on Gratitude* is its presentation of the Three Great Hidden Dharmas—the Most Venerable One, the Odaimoku, and the Precepts Platform of the Essential Section of the *Lotus Sutra* (see Chapter 2 for a discussion of these)—which had not been revealed since the Buddha's death. This work is the first explicit written presentation of the Three Great Hidden Dharmas. The essay concludes by stating that all of the merit accruing from Nichiren Shōnin's work as the practitioner of the *Lotus Sutra* would be transferred to his former teacher Dōzen-bo.

Other Important Writings

Treatise on the Doctrine, the Capability, the Time, and the Country

(*Kyō-ki-ji-koku-shō*)

Nichiren Shōnin wrote this work in 1262 on the Izu Peninsula during his first exile. This was his first presentation of his method of evaluating Buddhist texts. Known as the Five Categories of Teaching, it evaluates the profundity of particular doctrines; the talent, experience, and character of the people hearing the doctrine; the time when the teaching is to be presented; the place where it is to be presented; and the order in which each is to be taught. Based on these five considerations, the only appropriate scripture for this age is the *Lotus Sutra*. This essay also contains Nichiren Shōnin's earliest known reference to himself as "the practitioner of the *Lotus Sutra*."

Essay on the Title of the Lotus Sutra
(*Hokke daimoku-shō*)

Written in 1266, only a fragment of the original still survives. This was a letter sent to a woman who had formerly followed Pure Land Buddhist teachings. In it, Nichiren Shōnin discusses the qualities of the title of the *Lotus Sutra* in detail. He writes about the merit contained in chanting the Odaimoku and how a common person who chants in faith can still acquire vast merit, even if he or she does not fully understand it. The letter also explains the merit of the Odaimoku and why the Odaimoku itself is the ultimate Dharma. Only through the Odaimoku can women living in the Declining Age of the Dharma achieve Buddhahood. He strongly urges the recipient to accept the *Lotus Sutra* and to diligently practice the recitation of its Odaimoku.

"The Penal Pit Letter"
("Tsuchirō-gosho")

On October 9, 1271, after learning that he was to be exiled to Sado Island, Nichiren Shōnin sent this letter to his disciple Nichirō, who was imprisoned in an underground pit in Kamakura. He first expresses concern for Nichirō's health during the cold nights below ground. Then Nichiren Shōnin encourages his young disciple by stressing the merit of personally living the words of the *Lotus Sutra* by recalling the vows of the Buddhas and various deities to protect the followers of the sutra. He closes the letter by expressing his hope that he and his disciple will meet again soon. This letter has not survived in its original manuscript, but because it demonstrates Nichiren Shōnin's warm-hearted concern for his disciples, it has been widely copied and distributed since his death.

Essay on the Centrality of the Lotus Sutra
(*Hokke shuyō-shō*)

In February, 1274, Nichiren Shōnin was pardoned and his exile to Sado was ended. The government, wanting his advice on the Mongolian invasion because he had predicted it, asked him to return to Kamakura. On April 8, he was interviewed by the government. He did not speak of strategy and timing, of course, since he was a Buddhist priest, nor was the government looking for such advice from a monk. Instead, he addressed the causes for the invasion within the government's support of misguided Buddhist sects and rituals. Nichiren Shōnin thereby made his third appeal to the government to stop their support of these other schools and to put their faith in the *Lotus Sutra*. He soon realized that this appeal, like the others before it, would be ignored. Therefore, in the middle of May he left Kamakura and traveled to Mount Minobu. Shortly after he arrived there, he sent this letter to his disciple Jōnin Toki. In it, he teaches that the *Lotus Sutra* is the heart of all the sutras, that Śākyamuni is the most important of all the Buddhas, and that the Odaimoku is the Great Dharma which will bring salvation to all sentient beings living in the Declining Age of the Dharma. This doctrine is summarized in the Three Great Hidden Dharmas: The Most Venerable One, the Odaimoku, and the Precepts Platform of the Essential Section of the *Lotus Sutra* (see Chapter 2 for a detailed explanation). Nichiren Shōnin explains that the occurrence of the many natural and social catastrophes of the time and the suffering heaped upon himself are evidence that the essential Dharma and the leader of the Bodhisattvas from Underground are at work in the world.

"A Reply to Lady Niiama"
("Niiama Gozen-gohenji")

Nichiren Shōnin sent this letter from Mount Minobu to his follower Niiama and her mother O-ama in February, 1275. It begins with his recollections of his family home and his deceased parents; he was reminded of home because the two had sent him as an offering edible seaweed like that which grew near his home village. In the second half of the letter, Nichiren Shōnin explains that the Most Venerable One (see Chapter 2 under the Three Great Hidden Dharmas) preached in the *Lotus Sutra* is of unprecedented worth. He indicates that the bestowal of his Great Mandala, a representation of the Most Venerable One, plays a fundamental role in his doctrinal teachings. Because of this, he says that he cannot give a Great Mandala to O-ama because of her wavering faith, regardless of how great his obligations to her might be in other respects. To Niiama, on the other hand, whose faith was firm, he did bestow a Great Mandala. This letter demonstrates how seriously he took someone's faith. Sincerity alone, not payment, was his method of judging whether or not he should bestow a Great Mandala. This letter also shows the warmth of his concern for the welfare of his disciples.

"Letter to the Brothers"
("Kyōdai-shō")

This is another letter which survives in its original manuscript. Nichiren Shōnin wrote this letter in April, 1275. It was addressed to the Ikegami brothers, Munenaka and Munenaga. In about 1256, they converted to Nichiren Shōnin's school of Buddhism and had remained his loyal followers in spite of suffering many persecutions. Their father, a follower of the famous Pure Land priest Ryōkan, tried to force them to abandon Nichiren Shōnin. When he failed, he attempted to divide the brothers by disinheriting the older son and leaving all the family estates to the younger son in his will. When Nichiren Shōnin heard about this, he encouraged the brothers to remain true to their faith and to each other, and inspired them to cooperate in leading their father to the true path. In letters like this one and those sent to Kingo Shijō, we can feel the profound warmth of Nichiren Shōnin's feelings for his disciples and the wisdom of his personal guidance.

"Letter Regarding the Four Stages of Faith and Five Levels of Practice"
("Shishin gohon-shō")

This letter, which survives in its original manuscript, was sent to Jōnin Toki in March, 1277. It is a reply to his questions about the methods of practicing the teaching of the _Lotus Sutra_. Nichiren Shōnin explains the four stages of faith and five levels of practice presented in Chapter Seventeen of the _Lotus Sutra_, "The Variety of Merits." He indicates the role of the followers of the sutra in the Declining Age of the Dharma. He teaches that people in this age, having already established their relationship with Buddhism through written scripture, can attain Buddhahood simply by believing in and reciting the Odaimoku. The phrase "faith produces wisdom" states the fundamental idea of faith in and practice of the Odaimoku in our lives as followers of the _Lotus Sutra_. This letter is therefore one of the most important sources for understanding Nichiren Shōnin's views regarding faith in the Declining Age of the Dharma.

The Mount Minobu Essay
(_Minobu-san Gosho_)

This elegantly flowing essay, written in August, 1282, describes the quiet beauty of Mount Minobu. In it, one can sense Nichiren Shōnin's feelings about his final home. The letter concludes with a poem said to have been composed by his disciple Nichiji: "The passing clouds have cleared away, (leaving) uninterrupted winds of the Dharma on Mount Sacred Eagle."

"Report to Lord Hakii"
("Hakii-dono Gosho")

On September 8, 1282, Nichiren Shōnin left Mount Minobu on a trip to hot springs in an effort to regain his health. Ten days later, he arrived at the home of Munenaka Ikegami. The next day, he had his disciple

Nikko write to Hakii Sanenaga telling him of his safe arrival. Hakii had provided service, sustenance, and protection to Nichiren Shōnin during his nine years on Mount Minobu. Nichiren Shōnin wished to express his thanks and appreciation. He wrote, "No matter where I die, make my grave on Mount Minobu, because it is there that I spent nine years reciting the *Lotus Sutra* to my heart's content," indicating he knew his death was near. In the letter, he showed great concern for the horse which had carried him, for his compassion extended all living beings. This was his last letter.

The Preservation of Nichiren Shōnin's Writings

The preservation of Nichiren Shōnin's writings began while he was still alive. Many of his most devoted disciples began collecting his letters and essays to ensure that his wisdom would be available to later ages. Nichiren Shōnin entrusted some of his most important essays to specific people so that they would be preserved.

Jōnin Toki was one of the major forces in preserving Nichiren Shōnin's work. Nichiren Shōnin himself gave the *Treatise on Spiritual Insight and the Most Venerable One* into his hands for safekeeping. Jōnin also spent much of his life accumulating other letters that he had stored at the Nakayama Hokekyō-ji Temple.

Many Nichiren Buddhist temples have similar collections. The Nichiren Shu is sincerely dedicated to preserving these writings and making them available for study. Additionally, new writings and fragments are occasionally discovered. These are united into the collection when they have been deemed authentic.

Besides physically preserving the writings, Nichiren Shu's Risshō University, located in Tokyo, continues to study the writings with the benefit of the latest scholarship in Buddhist studies. The definitive scholarly collection of the complete works of Nichiren Shōnin (including those that have not been authenticated, which are noted as such), the *Shōwa Teihon Nichiren Shōnin Ibun*, was published by the Center for Nichiren Doctrinal Studies at Risshō University.

Chapter 6
Selected Writings of
Nichiren Shonin

Nichiren Shōnin's writings, as we have seen in the previous chapter, cover a wide range of subjects from doctrine and theory through simple, practical instructions on dealing with life in the difficult Declining Age of the Dharma. In the latter case, however, the instructions are not just religious guidelines. Nichiren Shōnin also provides his followers with practical suggestions on life in general as well as moral and ethical guidelines for living a gainful, wholesome life. His suggestions are so practical that his followers still find them useful today.

In this chapter, we will take a look at some quotes from Nichiren Shōnin's writings, and examine what they mean for us.

> Everybody knows that regardless of whether a person is wise or ignorant, high or low in rank, we are all born to die. Therefore, we should not be saddened or alarmed at death. I know this and have taught it to the people. Upon the death of your beloved son, however, I can't tell whether it is a dream or a vision.

This passage is from the *Letter to the Widow Ueno*. We all know that everyone who has been born will eventually die; the fact of death is not something to be feared or fretted over. However, the death of one who is close to us can make us wonder whether life is real or just a passing dream.

> Both the Mahayana and Hinayana sutras expounded before the *Lotus Sutra* preach Buddhahood in name only, without substance. Therefore the practicers of such sutras will not be able to obtain Buddhahood even for themselves, not to speak of helping parents obtain Buddhahood. Now coming to the *Lotus Sutra*, when the enlightenment of women was revealed, the enlightenment of mothers was realized; and when a man as wicked as Devadatta could attain Buddhahood, the enlightenment of fathers was realized. These are the two proclamations of the Buddha in the "Devadatta" chapter, and this is the reason why the *Lotus Sutra* is the sutra of the filial way among all the Buddhist scriptures.

This passage is from the treatise *Open Your Eyes to the Lotus Teaching*. Prior to preaching the *Lotus Sutra*, the Buddha taught for specific audiences at particular levels of understanding. They only show the possibility of enlightenment for those for whom they were preached, not for all people. However, the *Lotus Sutra* teaches and gives examples of even the most wicked person (Devadatta) attaining enlightenment. Furthermore, it promises enlightenment for women, something that no previous sutra had done. Therefore, it alone can ensure the enlightenment of everyone. By leading one's parents to a teaching that can bring them to enlightenment, one truly repays the debt that one owes to them.

> Disciples of the Buddha should not fail to feel grateful for the Four Favors (received from parents, people, sovereign, and Buddhism) and repay them.

This passage is also from *Open Your Eyes to the Lotus Teaching*. It reminds us that we must not forget to be grateful and fulfill our responsibilities. In particular, disciples of the Buddha should recognize their obligations to all living beings, to their parents, to their civil leaders and government, and to the Three Treasures of Buddhism.

> The first [of the Three Great Hidden Dharmas] is the Most Venerable One. All the people in Japan as well as the rest of the whole world should revere the Lord Buddha Śākyamuni revealed in the essential section of the *Lotus Sutra* as the Most Venerable One. That is to say, the object worshiped should be Śākyamuni Buddha and Many Treasures Buddha in the Stupa of Treasures. The other buddhas standing outside the stupa and the four bodhisattvas such as Viśiṣṭacāritra should be their attendants.

> The second is the Precept Platform based on the doctrine of the essential section of the *Lotus Sutra*.

> The third is the Odaimoku of the *Lotus Sutra*. All the people in Japan, China, and everyone in the whole world, regardless of being wise or foolish, should chant Namu Myōhō Renge Kyō singlemindedly forgetting everything else.

This passage is one of the most important found in the *Treatise on Gratitude*. This is the point at which Nichiren reveals the doctrines hidden within the *Lotus Sutra* for the people living in the Declining Age of the Dharma for the first time. These are the Three Great Hidden Dharmas. The True Dharma of the Declining Age of the Dharma is the Most Venerable One revealed in the essential section of the *Lotus Sutra* as the Eternal Śākyamuni Buddha sitting with Many Treasures Buddha and attended by the four leaders of the Bodhisattvas from Underground, led by Bodhisattva Superb Action. The True Dharma is transmitted at the Precept Platform prescribed in the essential section of the *Lotus Sutra*. It is transmitted as the Sacred Title (Odaimoku) of the essential section of the *Lotus Sutra*, Namu Myōhō Renge Kyō. See chapter 2 under the heading "Nichiren Buddhist Doctrine" for more information regarding the Three Great Hidden Dharmas.

> ...Śākyamuni Buddha's merit of practicing the bodhisattva way leading to Buddhahood, as well as that of preaching and saving all living beings since his attainment of Buddhahood, are altogether contained in the five words of myō, hō, ren, ge, and kyō (the Odaimoku) and that consequently, when we uphold the five words, the merits which he accumulated before and after his attainment of Buddhahood are naturally transferred to us.

This passage from the *Treatise Revealing Spiritual Contemplation and the Most Venerable One* explains the merits gained by upholding the Odaimoku of the *Lotus Sutra*. The Buddha has accumulated an unimaginable amount of merit over the course of infinite time. To become a Buddha, he accumulated merit by fulfilling the perfections of a bodhisattva over innumerable lifetimes. Once he became a Buddha, his merit increased beyond his previous merit because he taught the Dharma to save all living beings. However, the Buddha's merits from both his practices to become a buddha and his merits as a Buddha are transferred to us by the mystic power of the Odaimoku. To accept and keep Namu Myōhō Renge Kyō, reciting it single-mindedly, is to receive the boundless compassionate salvation of Śākyamuni Buddha.

> Those who spread the *Lotus Sutra* in Japan are parents of all the Japanese people. Grand Master Chang-an taught us that pointing out a man's mistake to help him get rid of it was doing him a favor. Then I, Nichiren, am the parent of the reigning emperor of Japan. For followers of Amida Buddha, Zen Buddhists, and Shingon monks, I am the teacher and master.

This passage is from the *Treatise on Selecting the Time*. In Confucian philosophy, one of the most important actions is serving one's parents. Grand Master Chang-an showed that correcting important errors is even more important than blindly following instructions. Since Nichiren Shōnin acted to point out the error of the emperor's beliefs, he was acting compassionately as the emperor's parents. Those who teach the *Lotus Sutra* in the Declining Age of the Dharma are teachers and parents to all people, including the sovereign. Because of this, Nichiren Shōnin can be identified as the master, teacher, and parent of the people of the Declining Age of the Dharma. These are the three properties that identify the teacher of the Buddha's Dharma according to the *Lotus Sutra*.

You should promptly discard your false faith, and take up the true and sole teaching of the *Lotus Sutra* at once. Then this world of the unenlightened will all become the Buddha-land. Will the Buddha-land ever decay? All the worlds in the universe will become treasure-worlds. Will the treasure-worlds ever be destroyed? When our country does not decay and the world is not destroyed, our bodies will be safe and our hearts, tranquil. Believe these words and revere them!

This passage is from the first of Nichiren Shōnin's five major writings, the *Treatise on Spreading Peace Throughout the Country by Establishing the True Dharma*. Having presented his reasons explaining that the *Lotus Sutra* is the correct teachings, Nichiren Shōnin exhorts the reader to practice the true teaching of the *Lotus Sutra*. It is important to do so, because our environment reflects our inner spiritual practice. When we uphold the *Lotus Sutra*, the sufferings of the world will be eased.

I have made a vow. Even if someone says that he would make me the ruler of Japan on the condition that I give up the *Lotus Sutra* and rely on the *Sutra of Meditation on the Buddha of Infinite Life* for my salvation in the next life, or even if someone threatens me saying that he will execute my parents if I do not say "*Namu Amida-butsu*," and no matter how many great difficulties fall upon me, I will not submit to them until a man of wisdom defeats me by reason. Other difficulties are like dust in the wind. I will never break my vow to become the pillar of Japan, to become the eyes of Japan, and become a great vessel for Japan.

In this passage from *Open Your Eyes to the Lotus Teaching*, Nichiren Shōnin explains that maintaining faith in the *Lotus Sutra* so as to be a guiding light to the people of the Declining Age of the Dharma is more important to him than anything else, including the most extensive materialistic power and the most intimate family relationships. This is because he has vowed to lead all people to the salvation of the Buddha Dharma. In the same way, we should uphold our faith without regard to material gain or loss.

With Nichiren's boundless compassion, "Namu Myōhō Renge Kyō" will be heard forever even beyond the ten thousand year period [of the Declining Age of the Dharma]. It has the merit of curing the "blindness" of all the people in Japan, blocking the way to hell. This merit is superior to those of Dengyō, T'ien-t'ai, Nāgārjuna, and Kāśyapa. Practice for a hundred years in the Pure Land is not worth the merit of chanting the Odaimoku for one day in this defiled world. Propagation of the Odaimoku in a two thousand year period following the death of the Buddha is not worth as much as spreading the Odaimoku for even a short while in the Declining Age of the Dharma. This is not from my wisdom; it is solely due to the time in which I live.

This passage is from the *Treatise on Gratitude*. Because Nichiren Shōnin has had the great compassion to teach the *Lotus Sutra* in the Declining Age of the Dharma, the transmission of the Three Great Hidden Dharmas will extend beyond the Declining Age of the Dharma into the endless future. The merits of the *Lotus Sutra* are so profound that it can open the eyes of those who do not believe so that they can also share in its merits. The merits of spreading the Odaimoku itself during the Declining Age of the Dharma is immeasurably deeper than upholding it at any other time, or of upholding any other teaching at any time. Nichiren Shōnin points out that this is not because of any special wisdom on his part, but simply because of the character of the Declining Age of the Dharma itself.

> Therefore, I urge you, my disciples, to practice Buddhism as preached in the *Lotus Sutra* without sparing your life and put Buddhism to proof once for all.

In this passage from the *Treatise on Selecting the Time*, Nichiren Shōnin reminds us that we should devote ourselves to the practice of the *Lotus Sutra* without regard for our material well-being. In this way, we can test the Buddha Dharma for ourselves and prove its power to others.

Many more of Nichiren Shōnin's writings are available in English translations. For a list of those that were available at the time this book was published, please see the bibliography at the end of this book. For a current list of available titles, please contact the Nichiren Buddhist International Center, whose contact information is listed at the end of the bibliography.

Chapter 7
The *Lotus Sutra*

Of the roughly 1500 sutras preached by the Buddha, the *Lotus Sutra* is the most important and the best known. The *Lotus Sutra*, like many other sutras, was originally written in Sanskrit. In 406 CE, Kumārajīva translated the *Lotus Sutra* into Chinese. While other translations were made over the centuries, Kumārajīva's version is still the most popular. In Japan, the *Lotus Sutra* has been studied since Buddhism was introduced there in the sixth century. Preeminent Buddhist scholars studied the *Lotus Sutra*—even those whose own doctrines were not directly based upon its teachings.

Antique sutra written in Sanskrit on leaves.

Nichiren Shōnin founded our school of Buddhism based directly on the *Lotus Sutra*. He devoted his entire adult life to propagating its teachings and putting those teachings into practice. The *Lotus Sutra* forms the basis for the fundamental teachings of Nichiren Shu.

The *Lotus Sutra* lays out the most important teachings of the Buddha. It shows us that we can put the Buddha's teachings into practice even in the midst of our less-than-perfect world. Furthermore, we can lead others to these teachings although they live in the delusion of the present world.

In this chapter, we will briefly review the contents of the *Lotus Sutra* so we will have a better understanding of exactly what Śākyamuni taught in it.

Chapter One
Introduction

Chapter One sets the stage for the story of the sutra. In it, the Buddha does not say a word. He sits in meditation at Mount Sacred Eagle surrounded by an assembly of all manner of beings: gods, humans, and others. Although some are the natural enemies of others, they have

gathered together peaceably to hear the Buddha speak. This peaceful assembly is a symbol showing that the sutra applies to all beings and unifies them.

As the assembly waits, a ray of light shoots out from a curl between the Buddha's eyebrows and illuminates all of the worlds to the east of this world from their lowest hell to their highest heaven. All can see that in each of these worlds there is a

Mount Sacred Eagle in India, where the Buddha taught the Lotus Sutra.

Buddha teaching the Dharma and leading the people from suffering. They can see people trying to put these teachings into practice even when being attacked by those hostile to Buddhism.

The assembly is amazed by this vision and seeks an explanation from the Buddha's wisest disciple, Mañjuśrī. In response, Mañjuśrī states that he has seen this phenomena before. The Buddha is about to preach the teaching that is the most difficult to believe in all the worlds. He wishes that all living beings will listen to him teach.

In listing all the various types of beings who are illuminated by the ray of light, this chapter shows that the *Lotus Sutra* is universal, a teaching that applies throughout the cosmos to all beings. Mañjuśrī's story of the sutra being expounded in the past just as it is in the present shows that its teaching transcends time. We also receive a preview of the Eternal Original Buddha who will reveal himself in Chapter Sixteen. The chapter hints at the idea that the Buddha's teaching of the *Lotus Sutra* is an event outside our normal concept of time and space. The Buddha is always present, teaching the sutra in all places, at all times, and at the same instant.

Chapter Two
Expedients

This chapter, named "Expedients," is one of the two most important chapters to Nichiren Buddhists. The chapter begins with the teaching that the Buddha uses skillful methods—expedients—to illustrate the truth. These expedients and the true teaching cannot be separated from each other. The fact is that the Buddha's enlightenment is almost impossible to express in words. The truth of enlightenment is beyond our normal experience. There are no words that can adequately describe it. Nonetheless, it must be expressed in words in some manner if one is to lead people to enlightenment.

The Buddha solved this dilemma by using expedients to teach, presenting portions of the truth in a limited form tailored to the group he was speaking with at the time. The sole reason for teaching in this manner was to lead all people to the same enlightenment as the Buddha. Because all of these expedient teachings were an expression of the Buddha's wisdom and compassion and were designed to communicate the truth of his enlightenment, their fundamental idea must be the same despite their apparent differences.

Chapter Two goes on to say that the *Lotus Sutra* is the ultimate teaching of the Buddha. In this sutra, he breaks the attachments his disciples have formed to his prior teachings. The Buddha states that all his prior teachings were expedients. They were partial truths that pointed to the whole truth. In the *Lotus Sutra*, these various teachings are unified in the One Vehicle, the Buddha Vehicle. The Buddha Vehicle teaches that there is only one true, perfect form of enlightenment, that of the Buddha. Anyone can attain this true and perfect form of enlightenment and become a Buddha.

> The Buddhas, the World-honored Ones, appear in the worlds in order to cause all living beings to open the gate to the insight of the Buddha, and to purify themselves. They appear in the worlds in order to show the insight of the Buddha to all living beings. They appear in the worlds in order to cause all living beings to obtain the insight of the Buddha. They appear in the worlds to cause all living beings to enter the Way into the insight of the Buddha. Śāriputra! This is the one great purpose for which the Buddhas appear in the worlds. [Murano, page 32]

Chapter Three
A Parable

In the first half of the *Lotus Sutra*, the Buddha uses three different methods to present his teachings to suit the differing capacities of the people who read or listen to the sutra. The teaching is presented in a theoretical form, then in the form of a parable, and then as predictions of future realizations of the theory. Chapter Two presents us with the theory of the One Vehicle—that there is only the profound enlightenment of the Buddha and that the Buddha is here to present this enlightenment to us. Chapters Three, Four, and Five illustrate the theory taught in Chapter Two with parables. Chapters Six and Nine contain predictions of the future. Chapters Seven and Eight have both a parable and a prediction of future realization.

Chapter Three presents one of the most popular parables, that of the Burning House. In this story, a man returns home to find his house engulfed in flames. His children are inside the house, but they are so caught up in playing that they do not notice the flames all around them. Although he cries out to them to leave the house, they ignore him. He then tells them that they should come outside because he has new toys for them: deer carts, sheep carts, and bullock carts. He tells them that they can have whichever they want if they leave the house. The children rush out only to find that they are each given an identical great white bullock cart, far superior to the carts he originally offered them. The three lesser carts represent the expedient teachings and the great white bullock cart represents the One Vehicle, which leads all from suffering to enlightenment.

Chapter Four
Understanding by Faith

In this chapter, the Buddha shows how we can believe, accept, and understand the teaching of the sutra properly. The Buddha leads all living beings by faith until they reach the final stages of enlightenment. In a parable, the bodhisattvas explain the principles that the Buddha has helped them understand. They tell the story of the son who wanders far from home, becoming poorer and poorer. One day, he returns to his home village but in his deluded state he does not even recognize that he has arrived at the door of his father, a wealthy man in the village. He is frightened that this wealthy man will enslave him. The father, recognizing his son, uses the ruse of hiring his son to work for him to prevent his son from fleeing in fear. After some years, he reveals to his son that he is in fact his son and heir. The father, who represents the Buddha, educated his son with expedients in an effort to raise his base mind and make it a noble one. This superior, noble mind is what we call the heart of the Buddha. Under the guidance of the Buddha, we are able to develop the heart of the Buddha, which all of us already possess naturally but are unaware of in our deluded state.

Chapter Five
The Simile of Herbs

This chapter presents the Simile of Herbs. The Buddha describes worlds filled with various types of herbs and plants, all different in name and form. In the sky above these plants is a large cloud, which provides them with water according to their needs. This simile describes the universal benefit of the Buddha Vehicle. Chapter Five teaches that though all living things exist at various levels of understanding, the Buddha provides his teachings to them equally in order to lead them all to enlightenment.

Chapter Six
Assurance of Future Buddhahood

As stated before, one of the methods of teaching in the *Lotus Sutra* is predictions of future events. This technique is used because some are unconvinced by only theory or parable. Sometimes a person needs to be told how the teaching will impact his or her life in the future. The Buddha teaches these people with predictions of their future as a result of following the theoretical teachings. In this chapter, the Buddha assures various of his disciples that they will attain Buddhahood.

Chapter Seven
The Parable of a Magic City

This chapter contains two entirely separate stories. The first tells of the previous existence of a Buddha named Great Universally Excelling Wisdom. This story, like the last chapter, is a "prediction of the future," but with a twist—the Buddha tells a story of the remote past, and the predicted results are occurring in the present.

In this story, we are introduced to Buddha Great Universally Excelling Wisdom, who was once a king but renounced the world, performed difficult practices, and became a Buddha. This Buddha had sixteen sons, who upon hearing of their father's enlightenment, renounced their positions and joined him as disciples. They along with all of the heavenly kings asked that Buddha to expound the Dharma and bring peace to all suffering beings. They said, "May the merits we have accumulated by this offering be distributed among all living beings, may we and all living beings together attain the enlightenment of the Buddha." This teaches the core of the Great Vehicle, that enlightenment is not individual but universal salvation. In response to their pleas, Buddha Great Universally Excelling Wisdom expounded the *Lotus Sutra*, leading many people to enlightenment. The sixteen sons all eventually became Buddhas. In fact, Śākyamuni revealed, he was the sixteenth and last of these, and therefore the culmination and keystone. This part of the chapter also foreshadows the second half of the *Lotus Sutra*, in particular, the Sixteenth Chapter. It indicates that the *Lotus Sutra* is the eternal truth, transcending the concept of time. The fact that the Buddhas of all directions attain enlightenment through the *Lotus Sutra* shows that all the teachings of the Buddhas are merged into the teachings of the *Lotus Sutra*. Finally, the central figure among these Buddhas is Śākyamuni, who resides in this world.

The second part of the chapter relates the parable of the Magic City. This story states that there was a city with great treasures. Many people wanted to go there. A guide who knew the way was willing to lead them there. The group set off toward the city. However, the road was long and full of danger. After a while, the people became tired and wanted to quit. The guide used magical powers to create the illusion of a city just on the horizon, telling the people that they would soon reach the city and could rest. The people were delighted. They entered the city and rested. When they had rested, the guide made the city disappear, telling the group that it was time to continue their journey. Having regained their strength, the people agreed and ultimately reached their destination.

The road to enlightenment is long and arduous, but we are easily discouraged. The Buddha, as an expedient, first explained the practice of śrāvakas and pratyekabuddhas. However, this was only a "Magic City" on the way, and was now to be discarded to continue on to the Buddha Vehicle, the real City of Treasures.

Chapter Eight
The Assurance of Future Buddhahood of the Five Hundred Disciples

In this chapter, five hundred arhats (those who have extinguished desire, which was considered to be enlightenment in the lower vehicles), including Pūrṇa, are assured of Buddhahood now that they have heard the *Lotus Sutra*. Pūrṇa was one of the Buddha's disciples and was considered the best preacher, distinguished for his eloquence. He could preach with such clarity that people could understand the Buddha's deepest teachings and free themselves from suffering. He went about preaching to the common people and did so well that he was able to assist many people in attaining enlightenment. In reality, Pūrṇa was a bodhisattva and practiced the bodhisattva way of assisting others to attain enlightenment. This chapter teaches us that anyone who would be a bodhisattva must also be a preacher, a teacher of the Dharma. If he does not, then he cannot help anyone.

This chapter ends with the story of the gem in the garment. In this story, a poor man meets an old friend who has been successful and is now wealthy. They eat and drink together, but the poor man, having had a bit too much to drink, falls into a deep sleep. In the morning, the successful man awakens first. He has to leave quickly on urgent business, but does not want to wake his friend. However, he wants to help his friend, so he leaves a valuable gem with him, sewn into the lining of his robe. When the poor man wakes, he does not notice the hidden gem, so he continues his wandering, poor and without work or a place to live. After a long time, he happens to meet his wealthy friend again. The successful man is shocked at the poor man's appearance. "Why did you not sell the gem and use the money to restore yourself to financial stability?" asks the wealthy friend. The poor man is bewildered, and then realizes that he has the gem in his robe. He had been wealthy all along, but never realized it.

This story is not about money, of course. Each of us possesses a gem of priceless value. We have the wisdom of the Buddha within our hearts, but we are not aware of it. This wisdom is the Buddha-nature, the potential to become a Buddha. Because of our deluded state we are unaware of our Buddha-nature and fail to make any effort to develop it.

Chapter Nine

The Assurance of Future Buddhahood of the Śrāvakas Who Have Something More to Learn and the Śrāvakas Who Have Nothing More to Learn

This chapter continues the theme of the previous chapters with more predictions of future effects. In it, Ānanda and Rāhula are assured that they will become Buddhas. Ānanda was the personal attendant of the Buddha and had an excellent memory. Everything the Buddha said, Ānanda would remember perfectly. Traditionally, he is considered the author of the sutras. The phrase, "Thus have I heard" that appears at the beginning of each sutra is understood to have been spoken by him when he first recited the sutras from memory so they could be written down. Rāhula was Śākyamuni's only son, born while the Buddha was still a prince. They are the last of the Buddha's followers from the two lesser vehicles, śrāvakas and pratyekabuddhas, to be assured of future Buddhahood. That Śākyamuni's son and his personal attendant are last indicates that there is no favoritism in Buddhism: all beings are equal in their ability to attain Buddhahood.

Chapter Ten

The Teacher of the Dharma

This chapter presents a dramatic development in the teaching of the sutra. Up to this point, the Buddha had addressed only those of the two lesser vehicles. From this chapter on, the bodhisattvas take center stage and the Buddha speaks to them. The title of this chapter is the "Teacher of the Dharma." A teacher of the Dharma is one who propagates the Dharma, the universal law or truth of Buddhism. Bodhisattvas are expected to propagate the Dharma. In this chapter, the Buddha states that if any person should rejoice in the Buddha's presence, even for one moment, at hearing a verse or phrase of the *Lotus Sutra*, he can assure that person of future Buddhahood. Even after the Buddha passes away, if one rejoices at hearing a verse or phrase of the sutra, that person will achieve enlightenment.

Up until this point, only those who heard the teachings of the Buddha directly from him had been assured of obtaining Buddhahood. The Buddha now assures all the people in the congregation of their future Buddhahood. Even more important for us, he assures us that even after his death anyone who rejoices at hearing the sutra will attain Buddhahood in the future.

After the Buddha passes away, the bodhisattvas play a leading role in his place. The bodhisattvas have the heart of the Buddha and their deeds manifest his will. This is why the *Lotus Sutra* entitles bodhisattvas to be teachers of the Dharma. In doing so, they should expound the sutra in possession of three qualities: first, the room of the Buddha, which signifies having great compassion; second, the robe of the Buddha, which signifies being gentle and patient; and third, the seat of the Buddha, which means having a mind free from attachments.

Chapter Eleven
Beholding the Stūpa of Treasures

This chapter opens with an enormous jeweled stūpa rising out of the earth and hanging in the sky. This opens the section of the sutra called the Assembly in the Air. Inside the stūpa is Many Treasures Buddha who comes and proclaims the truthfulness of the *Lotus Sutra* wherever it is preached. The Buddha summons all the Buddhas from the worlds of the ten directions (that is, the entire universe), purifies this world, and then rises up into the air and sits next to Many Treasures Buddha inside the stūpa. He then raises all the people in congregation up into the air so they can participate. After doing this, he asks if there is anyone willing to propagate the sutra after he dies and enters nirvana. He then warns the assembly of how difficult it will be to propagate the sutra at that time.

Chapter Twelve
Devadatta

Chapter Twelve is the "Devadatta Chapter," one of the most significant chapters in the first half of the sutra. The first part of the chapter discusses Devadatta, a cousin of Śākyamuni. Devadatta was an evil person, jealous of the Buddha's achievements. He tried to disrupt the Buddhist community (the *saṅgha*) and even tried to murder the Buddha. At one point, he started his own group, seeking to draw people away from the saṅgha. In all of the previous teachings, he was portrayed as the example of evil and depravity with no hope of ever escaping from the effects of the bad things he had done. However, in this chapter the Buddha reveals that in a previous life Devadatta had been Śākyamuni's teacher. The Buddha predicts that Devadatta will even attain Buddhahood in the future. This story teaches us that good and evil are not fixed immutable characteristics in people. Rather, they are characteristics that are developed by a person's circumstances. Buddhism believes that good and evil are not two separate things; there is no absolute or permanent distinction between the two. This chapter tells us that even evil people can attain enlightenment eventually.

The second portion of the chapter tells the story of the Dragon King's daughter. In this story, the Dragon King's daughter appears and then attains Buddhahood to the amazement of the assembly. In ancient India, women were considered inferior and incapable of attaining enlightenment. Śākyamuni teaches differently in the *Lotus Sutra*. He makes it clear that all living beings—old and young, male and female, human and non-human—are potential Buddhas. The enlightenment of the Dragon King's daughter also illustrates the concept of attaining Buddhahood in this lifetime. It shows that ordinary people have the ability to attain enlightenment in their own bodies during their present lifetime. However, it is important to understand that this attainment of enlightenment requires effort on our part. We must practice and apply the principles of Buddhism to our lives in order to attain enlightenment.

Chapter Thirteen
Encouragement for Keeping this Sutra

This chapter explains that anyone who preaches the *Lotus Sutra* in the future, the Declining Age of the Dharma, must have stamina. That person must resolve to propagate the sutra although evil people may try to stop him or her, and may even persecute the preacher. The sutra gives us an example of how we should live. We "read the sutra with our lives" by comparing its teachings to our actions. Whenever we reflect seriously on the quality of our lives, we realize that we often act in ways that are far from the spirit of the Buddha. We are confused by the illusions of the Declining Age of the Dharma. The *Lotus Sutra* warns us that this will be our normal state once the Buddha has departed from among us.

Nichiren Shōnin was the one who completed the practice of reading the sutra with his life by fulfilling its teachings and predictions in his deeds and experiences. The various persecutions visited upon him by the Japanese authorities caused him to rejoice in seeing the prophecies of the *Lotus Sutra* proven.

Chapter Fourteen
Peaceful Practices

This chapter is called peaceful practices. In Nichiren Buddhism, it is generally associated with the form of propagation called *shōju*, or gentle persuasion. The chapter describes the ways in which to preach and spread the Dharma when such a method is called for. Chapter Twenty, which will be discussed further on, is generally considered as the model for *shakubuku*, or breaking and subduing the illusions of people as propagation.

Chapter Fifteen
Appearance of the Bodhisattvas from Underground

The title of this chapter is "Appearance of Bodhisattvas from Underground." These bodhisattvas, who spring up from the space beneath the Earth, are not recognized by anyone in the assembly. They appear only in the *Lotus Sutra*. Śākyamuni reveals that they have been his disciples for countless eons. It is these bodhisattvas who have the qualifications to propagate the sutra after the Buddha's extinction. In Chapter Twenty-one, the Buddha will transmit the *Lotus Sutra* to them for that purpose.

Chapter Sixteen
The Duration of the Life of the Tathāgata

This chapter, the most important to Nichiren Buddhists, reveals the true nature of the Buddha and also of his true Pure Land. The Buddha announces that he is eternal, without beginning or end. Most people think of the Buddha as the historical person Śākyamuni who was born as a prince in what is now Nepal, renounced his throne, attained enlightenment, and thus became the Buddha. However, this limited

Śākyamuni is an expedient version of the Buddha, or a provisional Buddha. Chapter Sixteen reveals that the Buddha is actually an ever-lasting and immortal being, possessing eternal life. The main point of the *Lotus Sutra* is this: all Buddhas, whatever names they may use, are temporary manifestations of this Eternal Buddha. He appears in other forms in order to lead people to enlightenment. However, these Buddhas are limited. They are provisional, only a reflection of the true form of the Eternal Buddha Śākyamuni in a given time and place.

Śākyamuni announces that he is forever expounding the Dharma in order to save all living beings. Before the *Lotus Sutra*, the only part of the Buddha thought to be eternal was the Truth itself as an aspect of the Buddha. However, the Truth as an abstract idea like this is beyond our comprehension and therefore cannot lead us to enlightenment. Only when Śākyamuni reveals the truth in his actual person and in his actual behavior can we be saved by the power of his mercy and wisdom. The *Lotus Sutra*'s teaching of the Eternal Buddha brings together all of the aspects of the Buddha: the Truth, the person, and enlightened action.

We can see this complete figure of the Buddha when we faithfully devote ourselves to him. Faith in this case means devoting our actions and our thoughts to the Buddha's way as expressed in his teaching in the *Lotus Sutra*. The physical body of the Buddha no longer exists since his body passed away, so the direct object of our devotion should be his teachings in the form of the *Lotus Sutra*. This sutra is the spirit of the Buddha and, since the Buddha's death, his physical manifestation. Respecting and making offerings to the sutra is exactly the same as respecting and making offerings to the Buddha himself.

The second important point in this chapter is that the Buddha's Pure Land is not any place other than this world. It is right here, right now. The *Lotus Sutra* tells us that the World of Endurance is the Pure Land.

> This pure world of mine can never be destroyed.
> My pure land is indestructible,
> But perverted people think;
> "It is full of sorrow, fear and pain.
> It will soon burn away." [Murano, page 248]

Since the Original Buddha is eternal, this world, where the Buddha lives, is also eternal. It can never be destroyed. However, ordinary people, deluded by worldly desires and unable to see with the eyes of the Buddha, think that this world is a defiled land, one which will burn away in the future. We see grief, pain and fear wherever we look. To us this is the "real world." But our Buddha-nature can be realized in this defiled world. To enlightened eyes, the real world is revealed as a glorious Pure Land where all beings can attain Buddhahood.

In the final verses to this chapter, the Buddha says:

I am always thinking:
How can I cause all living beings
To enter the supreme way
And quickly become Buddhas? [Murano, page 249]

These verses summarize the chapter. This is the Buddha's hope for all living things: to cause all people to attain Buddhahood; to direct them all to the one Buddha-world; and to establish a perfect peaceful land in this world, so that absolute individual peace of mind and absolute peace of society are realized. These are the great purposes of the *Lotus Sutra*.

In Chapter Sixteen, the Buddha again tells a story to help explain his meaning. In the Parable of the Good Doctor, Śākyamuni Buddha tells the story of an excellent doctor with many sons. One day, the doctor goes on a business trip to a distant land. While he is gone, his sons decide to try out his medicines to see what happens. Unfortunately, they select a poisonous medicine, and suffer terrible pain and mental disorientation. When the doctor returns home, he finds his children suffering terribly and in danger of dying. All of the children are happy to see him since they know that he will save their lives. The doctor mixes up an antidote for them; unlike some modern drugs, his medicine looks, smells, and tastes delightful. Some of his sons take the medicine right away and are cured. However, some of his children are so deranged by the poisonous drug that they believe the antidote smells and tastes bad, so they are unwilling to take it. The doctor tries to get them to take the antidote anyway, but their minds are too poisoned to follow his advice. To get these sons to take their medicine, the doctor come up with a plan. He tells all of his sons that he is going away on another business trip to a remote land and that while he is gone, they should come to their senses and take the medicine. He then leaves and, after some time, sends a messenger to tell his children that he has died while traveling. When the children hear that their father has died, they are filled with sorrow for not following his instructions and are concerned that there is now no one who can cure their poisoning. In this state of regret, the children finally come to their senses and take the antidote. On hearing of his children's cure, the doctor returns home and explains what he did to all of his sons.

In this parable, the good doctor is, of course, the Buddha, and we are his children. The poisonous medicine is the Three Poisons of greed, anger, and ignorance that lead to suffering in the world. The good medicine is the teaching of the Buddha in the *Lotus Sutra*—specifically, the Odaimoku, Namu Myōhō Renge Kyō. Though the Buddha is always with us, when most people see him in the world they are unwilling to work to liberate themselves because they think that the Buddha will do it for them. Therefore, he appears to pass away in his physical body so that we will take the initiative and work for our own liberation.

Chapter Seventeen
The Variety of Merits

Śākyamuni Buddha says that the practitioners of the Dharma, even those who have just begun, should believe in and accept this sutra, despite the fact that it contains his most advanced teachings. In this chapter, he explains the merits acquired by simply believing in the truth of the *Lotus Sutra*.

The Great teacher Chih-i, the founder of the T'ien T'ai school that Nichiren Shōnin considered one of his teachers, described five stages of practice for believers in the *Lotus Sutra* after Śākyamuni died. The five states are: first, rejoicing on hearing the sutra; second, reading and reciting the Sutra; third, expounding the sutra to others; fourth, practicing the Six Perfections; and fifth, mastering the Six Perfections.

The first stage of rejoicing occurs when one listens to the *Lotus Sutra*, receives it joyfully, and desires to follow its teachings. At the second stage, a person who has already experienced the joy makes further progress, reading and reciting the sutra aloud, studying it seriously, and exploring its meaning. In the third stage, one is able to explain it to others. In the fourth stage, the practitioner has become so immersed in the sutra that he or she begins to practice the Six Perfections of the bodhisattvas. Finally, in the fifth stage the practitioner upholds the sutra in his or her daily life, plumbs its deepest meaning, explains it to others, practices the Six Perfections, and begins to see the Six Perfections arise naturally in his or her life.

The Six Perfections are considered the bodhisattva way of practice. They are **generosity**, the performance of service to others in both a spiritual and material sense; **morality**, living an ethical life by avoiding the taking of life, stealing, indulgence in harmful sexual activity, lying, or becoming intoxicated with alcohol or drugs; **patience**, showing patience in dealing with obstacles and opposition from others; **endeavor**, making the best effort one can; **concentration**, focusing the heart and mind on the task at hand; and **wisdom**, which is more than simple knowledge or understanding. The Buddha's realization of the Truth was wisdom. With this wisdom, the Buddha's person and the Truth are one: subjective character and objective truth merge and are unified.

Of these stages the first one, having a joyful heart when hearing the sutra, is the most important. This is when we take faith in and experience the joy of hearing the *Lotus Sutra*, practice it, behave as it teaches, and finally attain enlightenment.

Nichiren Shōnin considered this teaching extremely important. In his essay the "Letter Regarding the Four Stages of Faith and Five Levels of Practice," he teaches that the stage of rejoicing was the vital point in these teachings. When we begin to practice the *Lotus Sutra*, place our faith in its teaching, and receive that teaching joyfully for even a single moment, we will naturally desire to learn and practice more. Nichiren Shōnin taught that believing in, accepting, and chanting the Odaimoku, Namu Myōhō Renge Kyō, is the proper practice for ordinary people in the Declining Age of the Dharma. It is a practical way for all people, both beginners and long time practitioners, to practice the *Lotus Sutra* and attain Buddhahood.

Chapter Eighteen
The Merits of a Person Who Rejoices at Hearing this Sutra

This chapter explains the merits received by one who takes faith in the *Lotus Sutra*, rejoices in it, and begins to practice its teachings. The joy one experiences when taking faith in the *Lotus Sutra* is a turning point in one's life. It reinforces one's faith in the sutra and impacts all of one's future activities. The merits received in the first moment of joy are greater than from anything else one may practice. It is the key to everything else that follows. It puts the believer on the path to enlightenment. It is a simple step that anyone can undertake, no matter how limited or gifted. Therefore, this is the one sutra that has the power to save all living beings.

Chapter Nineteen
The Merits of the Teacher of the Dharma

This chapter speaks about the merits acquired by those who teaches this sutra. As stated before, teaching the Truth to others is one of the bodhisattva practices. Therefore, one who practices the sutra must also teach the Dharma. The sutra often says, "you should keep, read, recite, expound, and copy this sutra." To keep the sutra means that we should endeavor to accept and uphold its teachings. To read the sutra means exactly that, to read it. To expound the sutra means to teach it to others. To copy the sutra means to copy it or to cause others to copy it for our use.

As practitioners, we should constantly do these things. In this way, we practice both for ourselves and for others. This chapter tells us that by doing these practices we purify our mind and body. We can begin to see the world as it truly is. We can discern the good and evil in what others think and do. We are able to expound the sutra to others and bring them to rejoice at hearing it. Our bodies become pure and reflect the teaching of the Buddha like a clean mirror. Our minds become pure and allow us to understand the sutra's teachings and to teach in accord with the teaching of the Buddha.

Chapter Twenty
Bodhisattva Never Despise

This chapter tells the story of Bodhisattva Never Despise, an important example to all who practice the *Lotus Sutra*. Bodhisattva Never Despise would bow to the people he met and tell them that he did not despise them and that, some day, they would become Buddhas. This did not sit well with most people; at best, this seemed to be a backhanded compliment. They would chase Bodhisattva Never Despise, beat him with rocks and sticks, and insult him. He would flee from harm's way and bow to them, repeating that he did not despise them and that someday they would become Buddhas. Eventually, the very people who had attacked him and insulted him came to listen to him and were led to the *Lotus Sutra*. They would eventually be enlightened through his efforts in teaching the Dharma to them. The fundamental lesson of Bodhisattva Never Despise is simple: have respect for all living beings. This is the standard one must use when propagating the sutra, an attitude of profound respect for every living person.

Chapter Twenty-one
The Supernatural Powers of the Tathāgatas

In chapter Fifteen, we were introduced to the Bodhisattvas from Underground. Their leaders are four bodhisattvas, including Bodhisattva Superb Action who is the overall leader. They came to the assembly to accept the task of propagating the *Lotus Sutra* after Śākyamuni's death. In this chapter, Śākyamuni assigns this mission to them and then transmits the Sutra's most profound teaching to them.

The most profound teaching of the sutra includes all of the teachings of the Buddha, all of the supernatural powers of the Buddha, the treasury of the hidden core of the Buddha, and all the achievements of the Buddha. These are called the Four Phrases of the Primary Mystery. Nichiren Shōnin taught that these four are found in the Odaimoku itself. This is what the Buddha transmits to the Bodhisattvas from Underground, the core of the sutra manifested in the title Myōhō Renge Kyō. This is the teaching that the bodhisattvas should propagate in the Declining Age of the Dharma.

For Nichiren Shōnin, this event is of fundamental significance. First, Nichiren Shōnin believed that Bodhisattva Superb Action would appear in Japan to save its people. He considered himself the representative of Bodhisattva Superb Action and was very serious in attempting to fulfill that role.

> ... the sutra teaches that Nichiren Shōnin is the messenger of the Eternal Buddha and a manifestation of Bodhisattva Superb Action and the practitioner of the Essential Section of the *Lotus Sutra* and the great leader of the Declining Age of the Dharma. ["Kingo Shijo's Letter of Explanation," *Shōwa Teihon* page 1352, trans. for this work by Rev. Ryūken Akahoshi]

Of even greater importance, Nichiren Shōnin tells us that the scene depicted in this chapter, the transmission of the Dharma to the Bodhisattvas from Underground, is the Most Venerable One, the focus of devotion for meditation. All living beings should chant Namu Myōhō Renge Kyō and focus their devotion on the scene depicted in this chapter. This scene is depicted in calligraphy on the Great Mandala used by Nichiren Buddhists.

Chapter Twenty-two
Transmission

This chapter describes the general transmission of the Dharma to all gathered at the assembly in the sky. This should not be confused with the specific transmission of the Dharma described in Chapter Twenty-one. The transmission of the Dharma to the Bodhisattvas from Underground is given to the direct disciples of the Eternal Buddha. The bodhisattvas who receive the transmission in the present chapter are those taught by the historical Buddha Śākyamuni.

The Bodhisattvas from Underground have assumed the specific duty of spreading the teachings of the sutra in the Declining Age of the Dharma. This is a task for bodhisattvas of outstanding ability and patience, who are able to overcome apathy and the resentment of others. The bodhisattvas taught by the historical Buddha are assigned another task. They are to propagate the sutra in the two ages before the Declining Age of the Dharma or in other worlds.

Chapter Twenty-three
The Previous Life of Medicine-King Bodhisattva

This chapter discusses the accomplishments of Bodhisattva Medicine King. He has the ability to transform himself into other living beings. He can do this to show a physical form that is appropriate to the nature of the person to whom he preaches the Dharma. In a similar manner, we must be prepared to present the Dharma to people according to their needs and abilities.

Śākyamuni explains how the *Lotus Sutra* is unsurpassed by any other sutra. Only the *Lotus Sutra* has the power to save all living beings from suffering and to give them joy. He describes the sutra as the best medicine to cure the sickness of the world. This section describes the bodhisattva burning various parts of his body as an offering to the Buddha. However, this should not be read as literal instructions to set oneself on fire. Instead, it is a symbolic description of the spirit of complete giving of one's whole self, believing wholeheartedly, and offering to serve the Dharma with all of one's body and soul.

Chapter Twenty-four
Wonderful-Voice Bodhisattva

This chapter tells the story of Bodhisattva Wonderful Voice. In it, the bodhisattva travels from his mystical, purified world to this world of endurance to make offerings to the Buddha. The important teaching of this chapter is that the Pure Land of the Buddha is not some far away place. The Pure Land of the Buddha is found wherever the *Lotus Sutra* is preached. We encounter it right here in this world. It is here that the Eternal Buddha revealed himself and preached the *Lotus Sutra*. Even Buddhas and bodhisattvas who live in worlds that seem to be far superior to our world come to this world to pay him homage. Therefore, though this world appears to be the most defiled to most of us, to the enlightened eye this world is actually the most superior Pure Land.

Another lesson found in this chapter regards a bodhisattva's ability to transform into other living beings. When we sincerely devote ourselves to the service of and welfare of other living beings, we reach a stage of true selflessness and become one with them. We understand their sufferings and needs, their abilities or lack of abilities. This is an expression of the bodhisattva spirit of devoting oneself to the service of others.

Chapter Twenty-five
The Universal Gate of World-Voice-Perceiver Bodhisattva

This chapter presents Bodhisattva World Voice Perceiver, more commonly known by the Chinese name Kwan Yin or Guanyin. For many Buddhists outside the Nichiren schools, this is the only chapter of the *Lotus Sutra* with which they have any familiarity because of the chapter's contents.

In this chapter, Śākyamuni tells the assembly that if one calls on Bodhisattva World Voice Perceiver when they are in pain or danger, he will immediately hear their plea and free them from their sufferings.

In this world, all living beings are subject to the reality of birth, old age, sickness and death. Śākyamuni tells the assembly that Bodhisattva World Voice Perceiver can save us from the seven calamities of fire, flood, two kinds of demons, unfriendly rulers, chains and shackles, and bandits. In order to be saved from these calamities however, one must call upon Bodhisattva World Voice Perceiver with a pure heart. The Buddha and the bodhisattvas will only grant this benefit to people who are practicing sincerely. The Buddha makes this clear when he says:

> Lustful people will be relieved of lust if they think about Bodhisattva World Voice Perceiver. Angry people will calm down if they think about him and respect him. Perplexed people will acquire clarity of mind if they think about him and respect him. [Murano, page 317]

This passage refers to what are called the Three Poisons in Buddhism—greed, anger, and ignorance. The Three Poisons represent the mental sufferings. The seven calamities enumerated by the Buddha represent the physical and material sufferings of human nature. Material suffering is experienced because mental suffering exists as the cause of material suffering. If our minds are healed of the three poisons, we can expect that the material sufferings will disappear as well.

Like the bodhisattvas mentioned in previous chapters, Bodhisattva World Voice Perceiver has the ability to transform himself into different forms in order to expound the Dharma to people. As before, he performs these transformations in order to teach people in a way that they can understand.

For Nichiren Buddhists, Bodhisattva World Voice Perceiver represents a perfect bodhisattva who shares the same heart as the Buddha. He seeks to assist and save all living beings by whatever means are most appropriate for each individual. He is an example of the ideal that we should try to match when we deal with others.

Chapter Twenty-six
Dhāranīs

The title of this chapter, "Dhāranī," is a Sanskrit word that was interpreted in Chinese to mean "total upholding." This means to hold on to good and thereby prevent evil. Since it has the meaning of not losing the Buddha's teachings—the good—it signifies the memorizing the *Lotus Sutra.*

In the *Lotus Sutra*, one of the five practices is to recite the sutra, knowing it by heart and being able to recite it from memory. The bodhisattvas, as teachers of the Dharma, memorize the words and the meaning of the sutra in order to teach it correctly. The power of knowing the words of the sutra by heart is called the power of the Dhāranīs.

The great Indian philosopher Nagarjuna stated: "If a bodhisattva obtains the power of Dhāranīs, he will never lose the Dharma from his memory but will keep it forever." This idea, over time, came to mean that if we memorize the entire sutra and can recite it by heart, we will obtain the miraculous power inherent in the sutra. The phrases and words of the sutra are then called the Dhāranī-spells. In the *Lotus Sutra*, Dhāranī-spells are recited by celestial beings to protect the practitioners, teachers, and expounders of the sutra.

Chapter Twenty-seven
King Wonderful-Adornment as the Previous Life of a Bodhisattva

This chapter presents the story of King Wonderful Adornment. He had two sons who were in reality Bodhisattva Medicine King and Bodhisattva Superior Medicine. The chapter tells how the two sons wished to go and hear the Buddha of their time expound the *Lotus*

Sutra. Since their father did not believe in Buddhism, he would not give his permission. They decided to perform various displays of miraculous powers before their father to change his mind. Seeing these feats, he was amazed at their abilities and desired to know who had taught them these things. They explained that their teacher was the Buddha. This caused the king to accompany his sons to see the Buddha and hear him expound the *Lotus Sutra.* Because of hearing the Buddha preach the *Lotus Sutra*, the king took faith in the sutra, renounced his faith in other teachings, and was assured of Buddhahood.

Chapter Twenty-eight
The Encouragement of Universal-Sage Bodhisattva

This chapter presents Bodhisattva Universal Sage who appears to protect and encourage anyone who keeps and practices the *Lotus Sutra.* He will assist any practitioner in his or her aspiration to become a Buddha. Śākyamuni praises him for his resolve and tells him:

> Anyone who keeps, reads, recites, and copies the *Lotus Sutra* should be considered to see me and hear this sutra from my mouth. That person shall be upright and will not be troubled by the three poisons of greed, anger, and ignorance or any other worldly desires. That person should be considered to be praised by me, to be caressed on the head, and to be covered by my robe. [Murano, page 339]

This is the last chapter of the *Lotus Sutra.* When the Buddha finished expounding the Sutra, the congregation rejoiced, memorized the words of the Buddha, bowed before him, and departed Eagle Peak.

Chapter 8
The Practices of
Nichiren Shu

Practicing Nichiren Shu Buddhism

Now that we have looked at the doctrines, philosophies, and scriptures of Nichiren Shu, it is time to talk about the most important aspect of any school of Buddhism: practice. Buddhism requires regular practice; in fact, most students of Buddhism—including those who do not necessarily consider themselves Buddhists—say that Buddhism cannot be understood without at least trying the practice for a period of time.

In looking at the practices of Nichiren Shu, one should remember that some of these practices are either difficult or impossible to describe in words—especially, for instance, things like the pronunciation and rhythm of reciting the *Lotus Sutra* in the traditional manner. To learn many of these practices, it is best to have a minister or practicing members of Nichiren Shu help you. Also, as with any meditative discipline, the guidance of a person who is well-versed in these practices will be invaluable in understanding your experiences and assisting you in making further progress.

The Ingredients of Practice

Generally, the practice of Nichiren Shu is composed of several common elements, put together in different ways depending on the preferences of the individual practitioner or the specific ceremony that is being performed. At the temple, and occasionally for special services in the home, one will find other flourishes added for certain events. In Chapter 9 when we take a look at some of the special events and ceremonies, some of these will be described. In this chapter, however, we will look at the core practices as well as some of the more common secondary practices. The things described in this chapter include all of the elements and combinations that one needs for a complete Buddhist

practice, however—the remainder, which some people may find helpful or important, are purely optional and may be learned at the individual practitioner's convenience.

We can divide the elements that we are describing into primary
practices and secondary, or optional, practices.

Primary Practices

The most important practice for a Nichiren Buddhist—the only one
that is strictly necessary—is chanting the Odaimoku, Namu Myōhō
Renge Kyō. However, it is generally accepted that this practice will be
more meaningful to the average person when combined with the other
primary practices, and most people will find the most meaning in their
practice by adding some of the secondary practices. To learn how to
chant the Odaimoku, you need to hear others chanting and participate
in a group. Fortunately, there are various CD sets available that have
recordings of the chanting of the Odaimoku and reciting the sutra in
traditional pronunciation (described in the next paragraph). Ordering
information appears in the bibliography at the end of this book.

Of course, one might wonder why simply repeating a phrase is considered the most important practice for Nichiren Buddhists. Nichiren
Shōnin himself explained that the Buddha prescribed the Odaimoku as
a good medicine to cure living beings of the sufferings of birth and
death. To become more like someone we admire, it is helpful to act like
that person. If we want to become like the Buddha, we must act like the
Buddha. In the *Lotus Sutra*, the Buddha revealed that all Buddhas
including himself became enlightened by revering the *Lotus Sutra* itself.
This is what we are doing when we chant the Odaimoku. Through this
practice, we become one with the Buddha and cultivate our own
Buddha nature. This is explained further in Chapter 2 under the Three
Great Hidden Dharmas.

Another part of the core practice is reciting sections from the *Lotus
Sutra*. The most common sections recited are Chapter Two up to and
including the Ten Suchnesses and the verse section of Chapter Sixteen
(some Nichiren schools recite all of Chapter Sixteen, as do members of
Nichiren Shu on some occasions). Though at temples one will often
hear these recited in special pronunciation (described in a moment), it
is perfectly acceptable to chant sections of the sutra in your native language; in fact, it is probably good to do so occasionally. The basis of this
practice is the words of the *Lotus Sutra* itself. In almost every chapter,
the sutra describes the merit and importance of reading, reciting, and
copying the sutra. This practice also serves to inspire us with the words
of the Buddha in his highest teachings, which is only possible if we
understand the words. This is why it is good to recite in one's own language. However, when we are in a group of people who do not share

the same native language, we can recite the sutra in a sort of "universal" style—that is, the language in which it was traditionally recited in Japan. Most Nichiren Buddhists within any culture have learned this recitation, so that even when a group may not be able to verbally communicate in any other way, they can share the recitation of the sutra. This recitation is in a specialized Japanese pronunciation called *shindoku*; basically, this is the Japanese pronunciation of Chinese words. Recitation in this traditional style also serves another purpose. When we read the sutra in *shindoku*, we are actually reading the Chinese characters that make up the *Lotus Sutra* as Nichiren Shōnin read it. It is this version that Nichiren Shōnin, performing his function as the votary of the sutra in the Declining Age of the Dharma, interpreted for us. This is also the text that Nichiren Shōnin lived—the description of the bodhisattva actions that he emulated in his life and the prophecies that he saw fulfilled in his life were read by Nichiren Shōnin in these characters. Finally, the rhythm and melody of the sutra are preserved in the *shindoku* reading that no translation can capture. A description of this pronunciation is far too involved to describe here. Fortunately it is recorded on the CD sets mentioned above; the English translation is also presented on some of these sets.

Nichiren Shōnin spoke of one other practice required of Buddhists to express compassion and gratitude to our fellow humans; this is propagation of the teachings of the *Lotus Sutra*. There are two forms of propagation, *shōju* and *shakubuku*. *Shōju* means gentle persuasion, and is used to describe the propagation of one who sets a good example. People are naturally drawn to such a person, and seek to emulate him or her. However, the means that Nichiren Shōnin advocated for his time and for the Declining Age of the Dharma in general is *shakubuku*, which means to break and subdue. However, this does not mean subduing people, being rude and dogmatic, or breaking violently. Instead, this simply means to speak the truth about the primary effectiveness of the *Lotus Sutra* and to speak truthfully about the deficiencies of other teachings. This does not mean attacking people with an attitude of insulting their beliefs; Nichiren Shōnin says that the correct form of shakubuku is shown in the example of Bodhisattva Never Despise in Chapter Twenty of the *Lotus Sutra*, told in Chapter 7 of this book. Another good resource for the proper attitude to use for shakubuku can be gained by reading Nichiren Shōnin's essay *Open Your Eyes to the Lotus Teaching*; in it, Nichiren Shōnin does not denigrate the teachings that came before the *Lotus Sutra*. Instead, he recognizes each for its worth and place in preparing people for the highest teaching of the Buddha. However, he does point out in what way each of the teachings does not arrive at the complete truth. This is the essence of shakubuku: do not insult other teachings, but simply and respectfully explain why you believe that Nichiren Buddhism can offer a more complete vision of reality.

Secondary Practices

The most common secondary practice encountered in daily practice and in ceremonies is the addition of spoken prayers. The most frequent prayers are standard prayers; these express our desire for the well-being of all living beings, call on the presence of the Buddha and the forces of the nature, express our vows as Buddhists and as bodhisattvas, and offer appreciation to the Buddha, the *Lotus Sutra*, and to our teachers, especially Nichiren Shōnin. There are other standard prayers that are used when we pray for the sick, when we observe the death of someone important to us, and for special commemorative ceremonies such as the Buddha's birthday. Finally, sometimes special prayers are composed for extraordinary events; for example, after the terrorist attacks in the United States on September 11, 2001, many temples read special prayers for those who had died and for the restoration of world peace. The individual practitioner may also compose special prayers, or ask a minister to compose prayers, for special events in his or her own life. As always, the crucial matter is not the wording of the prayer, but the intent of the person who recites it.

As mentioned above, the *Lotus Sutra* tells us that we should keep, read, recite, and copy the sutra. Keeping, of course, means living by its example. Reading can mean either reading aloud or to ourselves. Reciting is generally understood to mean speaking the sutra aloud from memory. Copying seems obvious enough; but the sutra is quite long, over 300 pages in most English translations. More serious Nichiren Buddhists will actually practice the copying of the entire *Lotus Sutra*. Fortunately for most of us, Nichiren Shōnin said that all of the merit of the sutra was contained in its title, so most Nichiren Buddhists simply copy the Odaimoku, Namu Myōhō Renge Kyō, in Chinese calligraphy. This practice, known as *shakyō*, can be demonstrated to you by a minister or an experienced layperson. Other people will actually copy the whole sutra, or important chapters such as sixteen. The critical part of this practice is not how much one copies, how beautifully one can reproduce Chinese characters, or how many copies one can make. Instead, it is the sincerity and care with which we perform the task; we should do our best to be careful, we should not rush, and we should hold in mind that we are doing the copying not as a way to practice calligraphy but as a religious task. *Shakyō* is not performed as part of a ceremony, but it is often done on some of the annual ceremony days.

The practice of sitting quietly in meditation is often associated with the Zen school. Actually, all Buddhists have been sitting in silent meditation since the Buddha himself attained enlightenment. This practice helps us develop tranquility, allows us to gain insight into the working of our mind, and can encourage our efforts to be patient with ourselves. However, in Nichiren Buddhism, sitting meditation is always practiced with the chanting of the Odaimoku and reflection on the *Lotus Sutra*.

There is one final element that deserves mention because it is so easy to overlook. Though not a part of our ritual practice, it is very important that we, as Buddhists, express the virtue of generosity in our lives. Donation to a Buddhist does not mean only the giving of money, but sharing our time and compassion. Therefore, social action should be an important part of our lives. This can mean many different things—Buddhism does not impose political or social beliefs upon its practitioners. However, whether it is working to feed the hungry, supporting non-profit arts organizations, encouraging world peace and disarmament, or whatever cause suits our personal beliefs within the context of Buddhist ethics, we should reach out to our communities and give our time and energy to make the world a better place. This is, after all, the goal of Buddhism—making this world the Buddha's Pure Land and easing the suffering of all sentient beings. Consider working with your Buddhist congregation or as an individual in performing some kind of regular social service.

The Recipe for Practice

Now that we have the parts that make up practice, let's take a brief look at how these elements come together. You should remember that there is no one correct recipe; as in your favorite home cooking, the recipe is there to give you the general idea, but the chef creates a wholesome dish with some personal discretion. Therefore, although there is a standard procedure for ceremonies, they may vary from one temple to another, and individuals may do things differently in their own homes as suits their tastes and lifestyles. There are handbooks that outline specific forms for your home practice (for sources, see this book's bibliography), but they vary somewhat depending upon the temple that created them. Again, the form is not the critical thing, but your spirit while conducting your daily practice is important. The advice of a minister in developing a personal practice can be very helpful.

Practice in the Home

Possibly the most common form of personal daily practice is similar to a standard weekly temple service. This practice is performed at one's home altar, described later in this chapter. Several different booklets containing versions of the home service are available and are available from the Nichiren Buddhist International Center, listed at the end of this book's bibliography. A very common form is outlined here. The service begins by chanting the Odaimoku three times. Then, we recite a prayer in which we invoke those who are present in our lives whenever we practice the *Lotus Sutra*. This is followed by the verses for opening the sutra in which we offer our gratitude and praise to the sutra itself. After these introductory prayers, we recite the beginning of Chapter Two and the verse section of Chapter Sixteen from the *Lotus Sutra*. We then recite a brief passage from Nichiren Shōnin's writings. Then, we chant the Odaimoku—the amount of chanting is up to the individual, depending on his or her needs and schedule; more impor-tant that the amount of time spent chanting is that the Odaimoku be recited with deep respect from the bottom of the practitioner's heart. This is followed by the recitation of a brief passage from Chapter Eleven of the *Lotus Sutra* that explains the merit we receive from the difficult practice of upholding the sutra. Then we recite a prayer in which we dedi-

---

Basic Outline of the Home Service

Three Odaimoku
Invocation
Verses for Opening the Sutra
Chapter 2 Reading
Chapter 16 Reading
Nichiren's Instructions
Chanting of the Odaimoku
"Difficulty of Keeping the Sutra" Reading
Prayer
Four Vows
Three Odaimoku

---

cate the merits of our practice to our teachers, all living beings, and those who have died. This prayer also includes our prayers for world peace and our own improvement. Finally, we recite the vows of a bodhi-sattva and conclude by chanting the Odaimoku three more times. Some people choose to eliminate some of the spoken prayers or add others, but the recitation of at least one of the sutra passages (Chapter Sixteen if nothing else) and of the Odaimoku, of course, are always present.

Besides the daily practice, some people find it helpful to also do a practice known as *shōdaigyō*. This is a specifically Nichiren Buddhist form of sitting meditation combined with chanting the Odaimoku. Shōdaigyō has a standard form; very little variation occurs in this prac-tice from place to place. In this particular ceremony, the spoken prayers are generally responsive prayers when done with a group. The cere-mony begins by chanting the Odaimoku, Namu Myōhō Renge Kyō, three times and bowing to the altar (sometimes a full prostration, touching forehead to the floor). This is followed by a short prayer reminding us that the place of practice is the place of enlightenment, then by a statement of the Three Vows, much like in the standard home practice. This is followed by a period of sitting meditation; this medita-tion may be insight meditation with focus placed on the breath, or one may choose to focus on silently repeating the Odaimoku. This period of silent meditation may last as long as one feels is necessary to calm and focus the mind. The purpose of this period of silent meditation is to cleanse our minds and prepare our minds for chanting the Odaimoku. Next follows a period of chanting the Odaimoku aloud; in this form of chanting, one usually begins quite slowly and then slowly increases the speed of repetition until it is very fast. Then, the rate slowly falls back to the original slow pace. This cycle may be done once or several times.

Once again the individual or group returns to silent meditation, except this time the focus of the mind is definitely on a silent repetition of the Odaimoku, usually timed in some way to the breath. The purpose of the second period of silent meditation is to deepen our faith with the merit of having chanted the Odaimoku. Following this, the group leader or the individual recites the prayer for the dedication of merit, which is followed by a responsive reading of the bodhisattva vows and the vow to strive to uphold the Odaimoku. To conclude, one again bows to the altar as at the beginning of the service.

Other ceremonies and practices may be conducted in the home. Even those ceremonies almost always performed at the temple may be performed in the home for members who live far from the temple or for those who are home-bound for some reason. You can always talk to a minister about adapting ceremonies for your home, and even about developing special ceremonies for meaningful events in your life.

Practice at the Temple

There are a few differences between home services and services at the temple that we will note here. Usually, the service begins with the ministers singing prayers called *shōmyō*, which serve the function of the introductory prayers done at home. At this point, the sutra recitations are done, usually in the special *shindoku* reading since there are often people with several different native languages present. During the recitation of the verse section of Chapter Sixteen, the participants are often encouraged to come forward to the altar and offer powdered incense to the Three Treasures. This is done by stepping to the incense burner, bowing to the Buddha, taking a pinch of incense, offering it to the Buddha, sprinkling it on the hot coal within the burner, then bowing to the Buddha once more before stepping away. When visiting a new temple, you may want to observe the actions of the regular members to see exactly what their traditional method for this offering is.

After the recitation of the sutra passages, the chanting of the Odaimoku begins. This is usually accompanied by drumming upon hand drums. Though the drumming can be done at home, people living in apartments or with close neighbors generally save this for the temple to help maintain good relations with their neighbors. The pattern of the drumming is not easy to explain; however, when you do it for the first time with a group, you will find it quite easy and natural.

Following the chanting of the Odaimoku, the leading minister will offer the prayer dedicating merits. Then the congregation recites the bodhisattva vows (sometimes in the local language and sometimes in Japanese). The ministers end by singing another set of *shōmyō*. This is typically followed by a sermon from one of the ministers.

Some temples also alternate their standard services with *shōdaigyō* and other sitting meditation practices. Also, many temples have regularly scheduled study meetings. You should contact temples that you do not know the schedule for to find out what activity is going on when you plan to visit, as many have special events throughout the year, and do different kinds of services on a rotating basis.

Of course, temples also are the focal point for special services and commemorative events. The unique features and meanings of these services are covered in Chapter 9.

The Place of Practice: the Family Altar

As we have explained, Nichiren Shu practitioners perform a morning and an evening service every day. Going to a temple for every service would be the ideal situation, but that is not practical in our hectic everyday lives, particularly since outside of Japan, temples are often not close to the great majority of practitioners. Therefore, it is important to create a sacred space in our homes for performing services. These serv-

The Great Mandala of Nichiren Shu.

ices may be readings from the sutra or just the simple chanting of Odaimoku; common forms of daily services are described in the previous section of this chapter. One's prayers may last for hours or for just minutes. The important thing is that one practices consistently.

The area you designate as your sacred space is important in helping you to keep your practice and to help keep it meaningful. As you develop and change in your perception of the Dharma, this space may change as well. The Most Venerable One, or the *Honzon* as we will refer to it here, is the most important part of the family altar. In Chapter 2 and Chapter 4, the Honzon is discussed in more detail; the most common form used in the home is the Great Mandala. The Great

Mandala is a written depiction of the Eternal Buddha's Pure Land, the place were the Eternal Buddha resides.

A Great Mandala is usually given to an individual or family by a minister when the person has shown faith and has decided to become a member of Nichiren Shu. The Great Mandala is usually not given until several months after the person has started practice as a Nichiren Buddhist. Actually, all one really needs to begin practicing is oneself. Simply having a family altar is not Buddhist practice. One will not develop Buddha nature by just having certain things in one's house; practice itself is the most important part of being a Buddhist.

As the *Lotus Sutra* says, wherever you practice, the Eternal Buddha is present. Therefore, the place that you choose to perform your daily practice should be a place of refuge within your home. In this place, you can go to reflect on your daily life and work on yourself for your betterment and for the attainment of Buddhahood. Here, you can reflect on your community and the world, and offer prayers for those in need. This is the place where one practices and develops compassion so one can help others as well as oneself in walking the Buddha's path.

The ideal place for an altar is a place that is easily accessible to all members of the family. It should also be a place that inspires us to be consistent in our practice; as the saying goes, out of sight out of mind, therefore the altar should be in a "living" place in the home instead of in a forgotten corner. The placement of one's altar is different for everyone, since we do not live in identical homes nor do we have identical needs. Your space may be small, others may use a whole room in the house. The important thing is to create the space and to use it. If you are having trouble deciding where to place the altar, ask a minister or other Nichiren Shu practitioners for help.

The basic form of family altar

The most basic form of altar has the Honzon (usually a Great Mandala), a candle, incense burner, flower vase, a plate for offering food, and a cup for water or tea (see illustration on the following page). These objects do not need to be fancy; simpler may be better for many people.

The most basic items besides the focus of devotion for meditation are incense, flowers, and candles. These make up what is known as a "three-piece collection" and are arranged with the incense burner in the center, the candle-holder on the right, and the flower vase on the left. There is a slightly more full collection known as a "five-piece collection." In this case, the incense burner is in the center, two candle-holders are one either side, outside of which are two flower vases. Let's take look at the three basic items in a little more detail.

Sticks are the most common form of incense used, though powdered incense on a hot coal may be used at the temple, for certain ceremonies, or for those who prefer it. Keep in mind, however, that powdered incense needs to be refreshed often, whereas stick incense will burn for some time without constant attention—and, therefore, without possibly distracting one's meditations. The significance of burning incense does not lie in the offering of incense itself. Rather, it is the attitude of the worshiper, who wishes to mask other odors and by means of the fragrance create an atmosphere of sacred space. Typically, one or three sticks of incense are offered. In the Nichiren Shu it is traditional to insert one in the ashes vertically in the center of the burner, or three vertically in a triangular arrangement. The number of times incense is offered in powdered form during special ceremonies is either once or three times. In any case, it is not the number of times or the form of the offering which is important, but the sincerity of the offering.

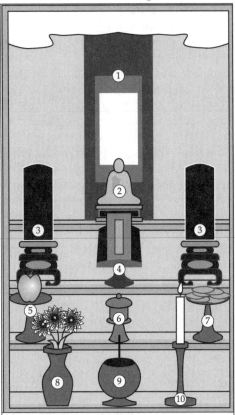

Typical Home Altar Arrangement

1. Great Mandala	6. Water Cup
2. Nichiren Shōnin Statue	7. Prepared Food Offering
3. Ancestral Tablets	8. Flowers
4. Ancestral Record Book	9. Incense Burner
5. Fruit Offering	10. Candle

Flowers offered to the Buddha on the altar should be fresh and not easily withered. Since the purpose of offering flowers is to offer the beauty and fine fragrance of the flowers to the Three Treasures, it goes without saying that bad smelling, thorny, or poisonous flowers should be avoided. Also because the flowers may draw someone closer to the Buddhist path by arousing thoughts of serenity in those who see them, the flowers are placed facing the worshiper.

Historically, light on Buddhist altars has been provided by oil lamps or candles; recently, electric lights are sometimes used as a substitute. Candles, however, are still preferred by the great majority of people. Regardless of the type of illumination utilized, each of these light sources produces illumination in the sacred space, symbolizing the enlightening wisdom of the Buddha. When extinguishing the candle, one should avoid blowing it out with one's breath, using a fan instead. Care should be taken after the service to make sure that the incense and lamps are completely extinguished, since they may cause a fire if left unattended.

Besides these three items, it is generally considered proper to offer water and food on the altar. The container for the water should be center behind the incense burner, and the food—usually fruit—should be offered on a tray or a small pedestal covered with white paper. The water should be emptied and replaced with fresh water every morning. The food offering should always be fresh and appealing.

In Japan and in Japanese households abroad, it is traditional to also offer tea, rice, and sometimes cakes. When this is done, the first serving from the first pot of rice of the day is offered on the altar. Also, the first cup of tea from the first pot is offered. The fruits or cakes should then be carefully arranged and presented on a pedestal covered with a white sheet of paper.

One final accessory is used during daily services: a bell and a wooden clapper for the bell. Their meaning and use is discussed below.

Miscellaneous Items

There are many other items which may be found on the Buddhist altar. These items are both decorative and symbolic. The Butsudan, a statue of our founder Nichiren Shōnin, ancestral tablets, copies of the *Lotus Sutra*, statues of protective deities, and decorations such as golden Lotus flowers, banners, and brocade cloth can be found at many members' homes and in many temples.

The Butsudan

The word "butsudan" means Buddha's platform. This is a cabinet used to hold the Honzon and to protect it from dust and similar hazards. It may be a simple box or a very decorative cabinet. Traditionally the Butsudan has three shelves at progressive heights.

The Great Mandala is hung on the back wall of the butsudan. Below the Great Mandala on the top shelf, one places a statue of he Buddha or Nichiren Shōnin. The next shelf down may hold ancestral tablets, a copy of the *Lotus Sutra*, and/or statues of protective deities. The bottom shelf is where one places offerings of food and water or tea. A small table in front of the Butsudan is used for holding the candle, incense burner, and fresh flowers. The bell sits on a small pedestal beside the table for use during the service.

The Bell

A bell is used in Buddhist ceremonies for several reasons. The most obvious is to mark locations in the service, such as the beginning or ending of the service and of the recitation of the Sutra. The bell is also a call to prayer—it tells us that now is the time for practicing the Buddha's teachings. When we hear the bell our mind is drawn toward our spiritual development. When used regularly, the sound brings our attention back into focus on the true nature of reality.

Statues

Many people have a very visual mind—that is, they find it easier to relate to a visible representation of a concept than to a description in words. Because of this, these people may find that a representation of Honzon in the form of statues speaks to them more than a Great Mandala. Often, the statue form of the Honzon consists of a statue of Śākyamuni Buddha, Many Treasures Buddha (the other Buddha who appears in the *Lotus Sutra*, beginning in Chapter Eleven—see Chapter 7 in this book), and a stūpa with Odaimoku on it. This representation is often found in Temples and can also be used in the home altar. Sometime, the Eternal Buddha Śākyamuni surrounded by the Four Great Bodhisattvas who lead the Bodhisattvas from Underground are used, as shown on page 14 of this book. If you have a Great Mandala you may want to place a statue of Nichiren Shōnin or of Śākyamuni Buddha in front of the scroll on a shelf just below it. Some people may choose to add statues of some of the traditional deities who serve to protect the Buddha's teaching and followers. One may see a wide variety of arrangements while visiting other members' homes and other temples. Talk with a minister or contact the Nichiren Buddhist International Center if you decide you would like to use statues in your home altar. Your minister will be glad to help you in looking for a statue to fit your home altar and in consecrating it for use in your practice.

Ancestral Tablets

Deep respect for and commemoration of one's ancestors is common in Asia. In Western cultures, this is not practiced in the same way as in Japan or in China, but forms of this practice do appear in our culture. For example, on Memorial Day the citizens of the United States honor their ancestors. Many people have recently have become interested in genealogy; this is also a way of honoring one's ancestors. Venerating one's ancestors is not necessary in Buddhism, but it can be a useful practice to develop compassion and to remind oneself that everything we have in life, including life itself, is the result of a long chain of striving on the part of others. This practice can help us forgive others and reflect on our own life, so we can continue on the path to enlightenment.

The tradition of performing memorial services goes back to the time of the Buddha. There is a popular story about one of the Buddha's disciples, Maudgalyāyana, who uses his supernatural powers to see what has happened to his mother after her death. He finds her suffering in hell, tormented by thirst and hunger. He tries to give her food and drink, but as he hands them to her, the food and drink burst into flames. Wondering what to do, Maudgalyāyana goes to the Buddha and asks for his help. The Buddha tells him to perform a service, making offerings for his mother and for all of those who are suffering in hell. Maudgalyāyana does this, and his mother and many others are freed from their suffering. This story reminds us that we vow to save all beings as bodhisattvas; when Maudgalyāyana selfishly attempts to help only his own mother his spiritual powers do not work, but when he works for the good of everyone who is suffering his spiritual powers are effective. So we pray for the living, but also the deceased, so all may find the path to enlightenment. In this spirit, some members may have ancestral tablets and ancestral record books on their altar.

In traditional form, ancestral tablets, or *ihai*, are written from top to bottom. They generally include the ancestor's common name, the Buddhist name (if he or she has one), and the dates of birth and death. Many Japanese Buddhist supply stores can create ancestral tablets for you in the traditional manner; some can also work with English lettering. Ancestral tablets can be expensive or inexpensive depending on the kind of wood used to make them and the artistry of the inscription.

Ancestral record books, or *kakochō*, list the names and dates of death for our deceased relatives and ancestors. In traditional Japanese form, these are fan-fold books separated into 31 sections for the days of the month; the name of each deceased relative is written on the day of their death. These books make it easier to remember memorial services for your ancestors. Traditionally, only ancestors are included in the book, but it is acceptable to add loved ones, friends, and anyone important in your life. The forms of ancestral record books vary from small and simple to large and ornate. There are different stands for these books also, from a simple book stand to a small decorative box resembling a miniature butsudan.

There are alternatives to the traditional ancestral tablets and record books. If you are a skilled woodworker, you can create your own ancestral tablets out of wood. A standing picture frame with a picture and/or the ancestor's name can also be used. A nice blank book can also be used as an ancestral record book.

The ancestral tablets and record book are by no means necessary parts of your home altar arrangement, but if you feel that you would like to remember your ancestors and loved ones this way, consider adding them to your home arrangement.

The Lotus Sutra

On many temple altars, a complete copy of the *Lotus Sutra* sits in front of Nichiren Shōnin's statue. When consecrating a Honzon, a copy of the *Lotus Sutra* is used to symbolically complete the marks of the Buddha, one of which is his far-reaching voice, or ability to teach many people. The *Lotus Sutra* is the perfect representation of the Buddha's teaching, the only one of the Buddha's marks that does not normally appear on a statue; thus the addition of the sutra turns the object of art into a Honzon. Many forms of the sutra are manufactured and can be used for the altar. The most common form for the altar is eight scrolls, because originally the *Lotus Sutra* was divided into eight volumes. When a statue of Nichiren Shōnin is included in the altar arrangement, it is usually shown holding one of the scrolls from the *Lotus Sutra*.

Golden Lotus Flowers and Other Decorations

Another relatively common accessory is a set of golden lotus flowers placed on the altar. These have several symbolic meanings. They are a reminder of the cycle of birth and death. There will be one lotus as a bud (birth), another in full bloom (life), one which has lost some of its petals (old age), and then a pod. The pod is the end of the flower, or death, but it also contains the beginning of another lotus—the seed within—that renews the cycle.

Various other decorations can be found on temple altars and, of course, smaller versions of almost all of these items can be found on some home altars. Common decorations include decorative lanterns, banners, brocade altar cloths, and different kinds of trays for offerings. Create your family altar to reflect what you and your family find inspiring in your sacred space. The point of the family altar, no matter how simple or complex, is to encourage yourself and your family to consistently practice the Buddha's teachings. Even the simplest altar can be an inspiration if it is designed sincerely with an open heart.

Buddhist Accessories

There are several other items used by Nichiren Buddhists in their practice wherever they may be: at the temple, at the home altar, or in any place where they wish to practice. Some serve special ritual functions, some identify one as a Buddhist, and some are aids to Buddhist practice; usually these implements combine these functions. Among those listed below, the juzu beads are an accessory common to all Buddhists, while the rest are unique to Nichiren Buddhism.

Juzu Beads

Juzu, literally "number beads," consists of a fixed number of beads threaded on a string. They are also called "thought beads" because they are used to remember the number of times one has read, chanted, or reflected on the Sutra. Juzu are probably the most widely distributed of all articles of Buddhist worship, and are even used by some non-Buddhists as a fashion accessory.

The traditional origin of juzu is ascribed to the following story of the Buddha. The king of Vaiśālī, a small country in India during the Buddha's life, visited the Buddha for advice. He explained that his country was small, so bandits raided with impunity, epidemics ran rampant, and the citizens knew neither peace nor security. He begged the Buddha to give him a teaching that he and his people could practice to relieve them from their problems. Śākyamuni told him, "Make a string of 108 nuts of the soapberry tree, keep it always with you, and count on it every time you chant the name of the Buddha. When you have chanted 200,000 times, you will experience tranquility of body and mind, harmony in the environment, peace in the nation, and happiness in your home. When you have chanted a million times, you will sever the 108 passions which are inherent in every living being." Having said this, Śākyamuni gave the king a juzu. The king had a thousand more made from the nuts of the soapberry tree and distributed them among his family and followers. From then on, the king always kept the juzu in hand, and every time he thought the name of the Buddha, his kingdom became slightly more peaceful. Finally, we are told, he realized the path of Buddhism. Since that time, Buddhists have carried juzu with them and used them to count their devotions.

Of course, this is not the real reason we use juzu. The juzu serves to remind us, like a string around the finger, that we are striving to live according the Buddha's teaching. For instance, when anger strikes us, we can grab our juzu and count out several repetitions of the Odaimoku instead of lashing out. They also serve to let others know we are Buddhists, and hopefully to inspire them to join us on the path of Buddhism. Of course, we also use them to keep track of our devotions.

As in the story, the standard number of beads in a juzu is 108; this number represents the 108 passions that are traditionally ascribed to the average person. However, juzu consisting of ten times the normal number of beads, or 1,080; half the normal, or 54; and half of that number, or 27, can also be found. The materials used to make juzu are also numerous; common materials include gold, silver, copper, crystal, soapberry nuts, bodhi-nuts, lotus seeds, sandalwood, and plum wood.

Generally the juzu is worn dangling in two loops from the left wrist. When the hands are joined in prayer, the gesture known as gasshō, the juzu hangs in two loops from between the thumb and forefinger. When reading prayers, reciting the sutra, or chanting the Odaimoku, one twists the juzu to make a figure eight that hangs from the middle finger of each hand; the beads then hang between the hands and the tassels outside the hands. The side with two tassels is held in the right hand and the side with three tassels in the left.

The juzu is not only for use in Buddhist ceremonies. It should be carried at all times, either on one's person or in one's pocket, brief case, or purse. There are many stories of the protective powers of the juzu—like a good luck charm—but the primary reason for carrying them is to help us keep our Buddhist practice in mind.

The Mokushō

The mokushō, or wooden clapper, is a unique Nichiren Buddhism accessory. This item is used to keep time while reading the *Lotus Sutra* and chanting the Odaimoku. The mokushō developed very recently, dating back only to Arai Nissatsu (1830-1888), who took a section of thick-stemmed bamboo, sliced off the bottom half, fixed it firmly in place, and proceeded to strike it with the end of his fan. Later, with the use of different types of wood, the tone of the mokushō became brighter and crisper. With this innovation, it came to be used at some temples in place of more traditional methods of keeping the congregation in time. Now it is sometimes even found at family altars for use during the family's daily services.

The Hand Drum

Like the mokushō, the hand drum is unique to Nichiren Buddhism. The drum-head is stretched tightly over a round frame, and is struck with a stick is to measure the rhythm for chanting the *Lotus Sutra* and the Odaimoku. It is used on many occasions, especially when the participants are walking or marching. From woodblock prints made during the Edo period depicting groups of believers carrying these drums as they walked the streets of Tokyo, we can see that Nichiren Buddhism adopted these drums in the middle of the nineteenth century at the very latest.

The Bokken

Another item unique to Nichiren Buddhism is the wooden ornamental sword, or *bokken*, which is awarded to and used only by ministers who have completed a rigorous ascetic training program. This sword, the use of which symbolizes cleaving asunder the clouds of ignorance, has a long history in Nichiren Buddhism. The minister holds the sword in one hand while conducting special prayer services, the *kitō* prayers described in Chapter 9, praying that we may cut through the clouds of ignorance and be embraced in the compassion of the Buddha.

Chapter 9
Events and Ceremonies

Nichiren Buddhism celebrates several holidays throughout the year, derived both from general Buddhist celebrations and from events specific to itself. Also, like most other religions, there are special ceremonies performed that mark the passage of milestones in one's personal life, such as conversion to the faith and weddings. While many of these can be celebrated as much at home as anywhere else, most followers participate in these events among their community of Buddhists at the temple. You can gain encouragement and a sense of integration within the world by sharing the celebration of landmarks in the year and in your life with your fellow Buddhists.

We will briefly discuss the major events and ceremonies below. However, you should remember that often a temple will hold the annual events on a day close to the actual date to conform to the usual temple schedule. Also, some temples may observe other events related to their community and the capabilities of their ministers.

Annual Events

Nirvana Day

On February 15, we remember the anniversary of Śākyamuni Buddha's entrance into final Nirvana, the day on which the historical Buddha died. It is one of the three major observances traditionally celebrated in honor of the Buddha by Buddhists all over the world.

One of the special elements of this event is the representation of the Buddha's nirvana. Śākyamuni is depicted lying between two *sala* trees with his head to the north and his face looking to the west, laying on his right side. He is surrounded by his disciples, protective beings, and every kind of living being, all sorrowed by their loss. This image of the reclining Buddha has been worshipped since ancient times and can be seen all over Asia.

The Founder's Birthday

Celebrated on February 16, this service marks Nichiren Shōnin's birth in 1222. Tradition says that the day Nichiren Shōnin was born, blue lotuses blossomed in the waves of the nearby sea and a fresh pure water spring appeared in the his parent's garden.

The Spring and Autumn Higan Services

The word *higan* means to arrive at the "other shore"—that is, to cross from "this shore," this world where we are immersed in the sufferings of birth and death, to the "other shore," where the Buddha resides eternally in his Pure Land. The week-long observance of Higan is a natural outgrowth of the Buddhist goal to escape from the world of illusion in order to arrive at the "other shore," the world of enlightenment. Therefore, the seven days of Higan, besides being a time in which to remember our ancestors and deceased relatives, is also a time to pray for our own enlightenment.

These week-long ceremonies are centered on the spring and autumn equinoxes. Generally, they consist of special Higan services at the temples. In Japan and Japanese communities abroad, families often visit the graves of their ancestors and make offerings of special Higan dumplings and flowers on their home altars.

The Buddha's Birthday

On April 8, we celebrate of the birth of Śākyamuni, who would become the Buddha. According to the oldest stories, he was born in the beautifully blossoming park at Lumbini. Immediately after his birth, the Buddha stood up, took seven steps, pointed to the sky above and the earth below, and announced, "I alone am honored in heaven and on earth." In remembrance of this event, Buddhists annually reconstruct this scene by building a beautiful "flower shrine" in front of the temple's main altar and placing a statue of the infant Buddha within.

Tradition further tells us that the Dragon King drew scented water from the air and washed Śākyamuni's body at the moment of his birth. Because of this, the celebration of the Buddha's Birthday has come to include the pouring of sweet tea over the image of the Buddha.

Proclamation Day

On April 28, in the spring of 1253, when Nichiren Shōnin was thirty-two years old, he returned to his home temple at Seichōji. Arising before dawn, he climbed to the top of a hill called Asahigamori and faced the rising sun as it gradually thrust aside the darkness over the Pacific Ocean to bathe the world in light. At that moment, he proclaimed to the world the fruit of his enlightened understanding, the Odaimoku, Namu Myōhō

Visitors at the gate to Seichoji.

Renge Kyō. On this day, we celebrate the founding of Nichiren Buddhism by chanting the Odaimoku as much as possible.

Obon

The official name of this service is *Urabon*, but it is commonly referred to as the *Obon* ceremony. Like the Higan services, this commemoration is performed in memory of our ancestors and deceased relatives. It generally begins on July 13 and ends on the 16th, but some temples calculate the dates based on the lunar calendar.

The source of *Urabon* can be found in the *Sutra of the Service for the Deceased*. In this sutra, Maudgalyāyana was distressed to discover that his mother was suffering in an unhappy state after death. He asked the Buddha if anything could be done to help her. The Buddha told him that on the fifteenth day of the seventh month he should make offerings of food and drink for his mother and pray for all deceased believers wherever they might be. These combined offerings, he said, would solve her problem. According to the sutra, Maudgalyāyana did as he was instructed and succeeded in leading the spirit of his mother out the hell realm and into the Pure Land of Mount Sacred Eagle.

The teachings of this sutra eventually produced the ceremonies associated with the season of Obon. Nichiren Shōnin referred to it in a letter sent to the grandmother of Nichii, known as the *Urabon-goshō*. He cites the story and uses it as the basis for his explanation of the origin and value of this celebration.

Commemorations of Persecutions

Nichiren Shōnin spent his entire adult life enduring political oppression and attacks from those who considered him a heretic. We remember his trials with Commemoration Services for the four most serious assaults on his life and safety: the Izu Exile on May 12, the Matsubagayatsu Persecution on August 27, the Tatsunokuchi Persecution on September 12, and the Komatsubara Persecution on November 11. See the story of Nichiren Shōnin's life in Chapter 4 for more information about these persecutions.

Nichiren Shōnin's Parinirvana Day

This observance, also known as Oeshiki, commemorates Nichiren Shōnin's death at the estate of Munenaka Ikegami (in present-day Tokyo) on October 13, 1282. At many temples, it consists of a simple memorial service for the founder. However, some temples conduct large celebrations, some lasting for several days. The largest and most spectacular of these ceremonies is held from the eleventh to the thirteenth of October at the Hommon-ji Temple in Ikegami, Tokyo. It reaches its climax on the evening of the twelfth, the eve of Nichiren Shōnin's death. Tradition says that at the moment of Nichiren Shōnin's death, the cherry trees in the garden blossomed out of season, and Nisshō, Nichiren Shōnin's senior disciple, tolled a bell to broadcast the news of his master's death. That is why today a "lantern offering" service is conducted with lavish decorations of beautiful artificial cherry blossoms, and a bell is tolled at the hour of his death.

Special Ceremonies

Conversion Ceremony

Many people consider themselves to belong to the faith of their parents, traditions that they have known since they were infants. Despite that fact, it is not uncommon for religions to conduct ceremonies officially bringing people into the community when they have reached a point in their lives—a specific age or an unspecified moment of acceptance—when they become officially members of the faithful. Nichiren Buddhism is no different. When a person decides to become a member of Nichiren Shu, a conversion ceremony is held at the temple. In this ceremony, the person takes refuge in the Three Treasures of Buddhism: the Buddha, the Dharma (the Buddha's teachings), and the Saṅgha (the community of Buddhists). Then, the newly converted person vows to uphold the Odaimoku, Namu Myōhō Renge Kyō, for his or her whole life. Sometimes a recitation of selected passages of the *Lotus Sutra* is included in this ceremony.

Receiving a Buddhist Name

In ancient times, people changed names whenever a significant event occurred in their lives. Nichiren Shōnin, for instance, was born Zennichi-maro and went through several names as he entered a temple to study, became a novice priest, took the full ordination, and finally when he proclaimed the Odaimoku and named himself Nichiren. A devout Buddhist will often take a Buddhist name to signify his or her commitment to living according to the teachings of the Buddha. It can only be given to a practicing Buddhist. Also, in a traditional funeral service, the Buddhist name is used during the memorial prayers.

Wedding Ceremony

One of the most common ceremonies among religions is the ritual that brings together two people who love one another. In Nichiren Shu, this ceremony can take many forms, from the most traditional Japanese ceremony to simple vows and chanting of the Odaimoku. The important part of this ceremony is not the ritual itself, but that the two people are committing themselves to one another before their community. There is no requirement that both participants be members of Nichiren Shu. This is a commitment to work to keep their love alive, to use their joined lives to serve the good of the community and the world, and to support one another in faith and in life.

Funerals

Funeral services are major events for Buddhists, as death is, with birth, one of the two most important events in a person's life.

The suffering of birth, old age, sickness, and death are facts of everyone's lives. No matter how developed science may become or how far medicine may advance, these cannot be avoided. Buddhism teaches, however, that when a person discovers that he or she exists within the life of the Eternal Buddha and can perceive the great stream of life flowing endlessly from the past through the present and into the future, he or she will escape the suffering that these events normally cause.

In Buddhism, the funeral service is accepted as just one event in the passage of time. Most Buddhists do not believe that everything about us ceases to exist upon our death. Death is the starting point of a new journey. Nichiren Shōnin taught that death is a pilgrimage to Mount Sacred Eagle—an encounter with the Eternal Buddha and with Nichiren Shōnin. The funeral service marks the start of this trip and aims at making the deceased person's journey a tranquil one.

Like weddings, the form of funeral services can vary quite a bit between different temples and depending on the wishes of the deceased and his or her family. However, there are certain traditions unique to Nichiren Shu that are often a part of these ceremonies. A special funeral robe with a passage from the *Lotus Sutra* or Nichiren Shōnin's writings may be used; some people have these made long before their death and bring these robes with them whenever they visit a temple to have it marked with each temple's seal. Devout believers who are aware that their time of death is near may have a priest come to their side to recite passages from the *Lotus Sutra* to help ease their passing. During the funeral service itself, the Buddha, Nichiren Shōnin, other followers of the Buddha, and the protective deities of the Dharma who promised to protect followers of the *Lotus Sutra* are invoked to ease the passage of the deceased. The minister at the temple is an important resource for those who have lost a loved one; he or she can assist with the sometimes complicated preparation process—both the legal and religious formalities—and can provide encouragement and solace to those who are left behind.

An poem written by the classic Japanese poet Matsuo Bashō when he was contemplating his approaching death says:

> The fallen cherry blossoms,
> The remaining cherry blossoms,
> Both, fallen blossoms.

We should realize that we are the remaining cherry blossoms that also must fall some day. In this way, we can recognize the fact that a funeral service is not only for the benefit of the deceased, but for all the living participants as well.

Memorial Services

Memorial services for deceased relatives have been a part of Japanese culture almost since the beginning of recorded history. Many outside observers have attributed this tradition to a cultural tendency toward ancestor worship; however, this is not entirely accurate. The source of these traditions is not to worship one's ancestors, but instead to be mindful of the gratitude we owe to those who came before us, without which we would not exist. In either case, the importance that is placed on these services in traditional Japanese communities is beginning to decline, particularly among those Buddhists who are not of Japanese heritage. Despite this fact, some observance of memorials for the decease serve a purpose, so these services should certainly not be entirely abandoned.

Like funeral services, memorials are conducted as much (if not more) for the living than for the dead. They serve several purposes within our lives. For one, they are a way to provide solace to us for the absence in our lives of one that we have loved. They also serve to remind us of the debt we owe to people and things that have passed beyond our perception; like the farmer who watered the plants for our food, our deceased relatives are not within the realm of our awareness, but they nurtured our lives and helped us to exist. Last but not least, these services again remind us that all things are impermanent; nothing remains as it is, neither our lives, our loved ones, or even our grief for those who have passed on.

Traditionally, memorial services are held at fixed intervals; however, a person may choose to observe memorials at intervals that are meaningful to the individual. The traditionally important observances occur as follows: every seventh day until the forty-ninth day, on the one-hundredth day, and every year on the date of death. There are certain annual memorials that are traditionally considered particularly important: the second, third, seventh, thirteenth, seventeenth, 23rd, 27th, 33rd, 37th, 50th, 100th, and so on. Keep in mind that the Japanese system of numbering anniversaries considers the event itself to be the first, so that the third anniversary in this system is the second anniversary according to Western numbering; however, you may again choose to use the counting system that is most meaningful to you.

Kitō Blessings

You may at some time or another encounter a special ceremony called *kitō*. These are a secondary practice that certain Nichiren Shu ministers have been trained to perform. Originally, these were meant to be "exorcisms," used to drive evil spirits away. Like many ideas in Buddhism, "evil spirits" are symbolic of deeper truths. The "evil spirits" that these prayers serve to drive away are actually the obstacles to happiness that arise in our mind as the result of the Three Poisons—greed, anger, and ignorance. Nichiren Shōnin himself said that daily life is an extension of our Buddhist practice; what appear to be worldly concerns are a cause for, a result of, and a reflection of our faith. Sometimes in our progress along the Buddhist path, the Three Poisons can interfere with our daily lives. This in turn can interfere with our Buddhist practice. Kitō serves to remind us and assist us in getting beyond the interference of the Three Poisons and moving forward in life and in our practice. They are based upon specific passages within the *Lotus Sutra*.

Chapter 10
Conclusion

In this book, we have taken a thorough look at the basic beliefs, practices, and guidelines of Nichiren Shu. There is much more that one can learn about Nichiren Shu Buddhism, but one should always keep in mind that the most important element of Buddhist faith is practice.

In Chapter 2, we saw that the practice of the *Lotus Sutra* must encompass the Three Kinds of Action: body, mouth, and mind. We also explored the idea of the Buddhism of Sowing and the Natural Transfer of the Buddha's merits by faith. Therefore, as Nichiren Shu Buddhists we should strive to practice the *Lotus Sutra* with faith by chanting the Odaimoku as much as we can. Our daily practice will nourish our own potential for buddhahood so that we can plant the seed of buddhahood in others.

While we practice for ourselves and practice the Buddhism of sowing for others, we must be careful to interact with society with respect and dignity, following the example of Bodhisattva Never Despising and the other bodhisattvas of the *Lotus Sutra*. When we live the sutra with the Three Kinds of Action, our faith will be deepened and others will become more receptive to receiving the seed of buddhahood.

We can truly change the world for good. This is the bodhisattva ideal: to save all living beings as we walk our own path to enlightenment. By following the teachings of Nichiren Shōnin and the *Lotus Sutra*, we can walk the Bodhisattva Path and transform this world into the Buddha's Pure Land.

Bibliography

Anesaki, Masahura. *Nichiren the Buddhist Prophet*. Gloucester, MA: Peter Smith, 1966.

Christensen, J. A. *Nichiren: Leader of Buddhist Reformation in Japan*. Fremont, CA: Jain Publishing Co., 2001.

Lotus Sutra, The. Translated by Senchu Murano. Tokyo: Nichiren Shu Shimbun Co. Ltd., 1991.

Matsuda, Ryūshō, ed. *Lotus Petals*. San Jose, CA: Nichiren Buddhist Temple of San Jose, 1995.

Nichiren Buddhist Temple of San Jose. *Lotus Seeds: the Essence of Nichiren Shu Buddhism*. San Jose, CA: Nichiren Buddhist Temple of San Jose, 2000.

Nichiren Propagation Center. *Dharma*. Portland, OR: Nichiren Propagation Center, 1981.

Nichiren Shōnin. *Hōon-jō*. Translated by Taikyō Yajima. Tokyo: Nichiren Shu Overseas Propagation Promotion Association, 1988.

———. *Kaimoku-shō*. Translated by Kyōtsū Hori. Tokyo: Nichiren Shu Overseas Propagation Promotion Association, 1987.

———. *Kanjin Honzon-shō / Nyosetsu Shugyō-shō / Kembutsu Mirai-ki*. Translated by Kyōtsū Hori. Tokyo: Nichiren Shu Overseas Propagation Promotion Association, 1991.

———. *Nyonin Gosho*. Translated by Kyōtsū Hori *et al*. Tokyo: Nichiren Shu Overseas Propagation Promotion Association, 1995.

———. *Risshō Ankoku-ron*. Translated by Kyōtsū Hori. Tokyo: Nichiren Shu Overseas Propagation Promotion Association, 1992.

———. *Senji-shō*. Translated by Kyōtsū Hori. Tokyo: Nichiren Shu Overseas Propagation Promotion Association, 1989.

———. *The Shimoyama Letter*. Translated by Taikyō Yajima. Tokyo: Nichiren Shu Overseas Propagation Promotion Association, 1996.

———. *Shugo Kokka-ron / Sainan Kōki Yurai / Sainan Taiji-shō*. Translated by Kyōtsū Hori. Tokyo: Nichiren Shu Overseas Propagation Promotion Association, 1998.

Nichiren Order. *Shingyō Hikkei: a Handbook for Members of the Nichiren Order*. Translated by Kyōtsū Hori. Tokyo: Nichiren Order, 1986.

Suguro, Shinjō. *Introduction to the Lotus Sutra*. Fremont, CA: Jain Publishing Co., 1998.

Tanabe, George Jr., ed. *Writings of Nichiren Shōnin: Doctrine 2*. Honolulu, HI: University of Hawai'i Press, 2002.

Watanabe, Hōyō. *A Phrase a Day*. Translated by Shōkai Kanai *et al.* from *Ichinichi Ichikun*. Tokyo: Nichiren Shu Overseas Propagation Promotion Association, 1986.

————. *Watashitachi no Nichiren-shū*. Tokyo: Sōsaku Shuppan Co., 1980.

Nichiren Buddhist International Center

The Nichiren Buddhist International Center (NBIC) distributes most of the books listed in the bibliography. In addition, the center carries all currently available publications of Nichiren Shu in English, as well as the service guides and CDs mentioned in this book. The NBIC can also help you get in touch with groups of Nichiren Shu practitioners in your area. Contact the center at:

NBIC
29490 Mission Blvd.
Hayward, CA 94544
USA

510 690-1222
510 690-1221 (FAX)

Email: nbic@nichiren-shu.org
Website: nichiren-shu.org

Glossary

Āgama period   *see* Hīnayāna Collection period.

Agon period   *see* Hīnayāna Collection period.

Assembly in the Air In the *Lotus Sutra*, the meeting of the participants in the air above Mount Sacred Eagle after the appearance of the Stūpa of Treasures containing the Buddha Many Treasures. The Assembly in the Air begins in Chapter 11 and ends at Chapter 22.

Bodhisattva   In Mahāyāna Buddhism, a bodhisattva is one who practices the Buddha Dharma not only for self but also to ensure the enlightenment of all living beings.

Bodhisattvas from Underground The bodhisattvas who appear in Chapter 15 of the *Lotus Sutra*. They are the disciples of the Eternal Buddha from the infinite past, and are the ones empowered by the Buddha to spread the teachings of the sutra in the Declining Age of the Dharma. Their leader is Bodhisattva Superb Action.

Bodhisattva Superb Action Also known as Jōgyō Bosatsu (Japanese) or Bodhisattva Viśiṣṭacāritra (Sanskrit). He is the leader of the Bodhisattvas from Underground. Nichiren Shōnin is recognized as doing the work of Bodhisattva Superb Action in the Declining Age of the Dharma.

Buddha   "The Enlightened One." The title of Śākyamuni in recognition of the fact that he attained the most profound and complete understanding of reality. Such a person has the ability to free all living beings from suffering.

Buddha nature   This refers generally to the potential for a living being to become a Buddha. Nichiren Shōnin realized that the *Lotus Sutra* teaches that all living beings have the complete Buddha nature. In Nichiren Buddhist doctrine, the Buddha nature is like a field that has the potential to grow Buddhahood within any living being. It needs to be planted with the seed of Buddhahood, the

Odaimoku, and nurtured with practice so that Buddhahood can actually manifest.

Bussho   *see* Buddha nature.

Butsudan   A cabinet used to hold and protect the object of devotion (usually a Great Mandala in Nichiren Buddhist homes) on a Buddhist shrine. It is Japanese for "Buddha platform."

Chih-i   *see* T'ien T'ai.

Daimandara   *see* Great Mandala.

Daimoku   *see* Odaimoku.

Declining Age of the Dharma According to Buddhist tradition, the period beginning two thousand years after the death of Śākyamuni. The time spans after the Buddha's death are sometimes divided into three periods. The first period, the True Age of the Dharma, is a time in which the Buddha's teachings are practiced correctly. In the second period, the Semblance Age of the Dharma, the Buddha's teachings begin to lose their true meaning because of the passage of time. In the final period, the Declining Age of the Dharma, the passage of time has practically eliminated the correct practice of Buddhism. However, the *Lotus Sutra* indicates that its practice can still be effective in this time when spread by the Bodhisattvas from Underground.

Dharma   Generally, the teachings of the Buddha. The Sanskrit word means "truth," "law," or "reality." The Dharma is the path that the Buddha prescribed in his teachings for his followers. It can also refer to the ultimate nature of reality.

Eagle Peak   *see* Mount Sacred Eagle.

Eightfold Path The guidelines that were set forth by the Buddha as the path to ending suffering. The Eightfold Path is Right Views, Right Thought, Right Speech, Right Action, Right Livelihood, Right Effort, Right Mindfulness, and Right Meditation. The word translated as "right" means mindfully attempting to align the steps of the path with the teachings of the Buddha.

Essential Section The Essential Section (*honmon* in Japanese) of the *Lotus Sutra* consists of the last fourteen chapters (as opposed to the Provisional Section (*shakumon* in Japanese), the first fourteen chapters). This division is based on the understanding of who taught each half of the sutra. Traditionally, it is said that the Provisional Section was taught by Śākyamuni Buddha who attained enlightenment in India in the fifth century B.C.E. (the "Historical Śākyamuni Buddha"). The Essential Section is said to have been taught by Śākyamuni Buddha who revealed himself to have been enlightened in the eternal past (the "Eternal Śākyamuni Buddha"). While both sections are important, the Provisional Section reveals truths that reflect the ultimate truth (this section is also sometimes called the "trace" or "imprint" section because of this), while the Essential Section directly reveals the ultimate truth that the Buddha's original enlightenment is outside of time or eternal (thus, this section is sometimes called the "original" section).

Five Periods   A T'ien T'ai doctrine by which the sutras are classified according to when in the Buddha's life they were thought to have been preached. These periods in traditional order are the Flower Garland period, the Hīnayāna Collection period, the Great Extent period, the Wisdom period, and the Lotus-Nirvana period. The Lotus-Nirvana period, being the Buddha's final and complete teachings, are seen as being his ultimate teachings both by T'ien T'ai and by Nichiren Shōnin. See the entry under each of the period's names for more details about each.

Flower Garland period The first of the Five Periods for classifying sutras by when they were thought to have been taught. This period actually only includes one sutra, the *Flower Garland Sutra*. It is believed to have been taught during the first three weeks after the Buddha attained enlightenment. *See also* Five Periods.

Four Noble Truths The most basic statement of Buddhist doctrine, and the first teaching of the Buddha after attaining enlightenment. The Four Noble Truths are: life is suffering, there is a cause for suffering, suffering can be overcome, the way to overcome suffering is the Eightfold Path.

Four Sightings   The four experiences that Siddhārtha Gautama (the Buddha-to-be) had that made him decide to seek spiritual awakening instead of continuing his life of pursuing pleasure. The Four Sightings were of an old man burdened by extreme age, a sick man tortured by his illness, a corpse surrounded by grieving family members, and a wandering holy man. Never having seen suffering in any form, the first three sightings inspired Siddhārtha to look for their meaning and cure, and the last showed him how to seek enlightenment.

Gohonzon   *see* Most Venerable One.

Go-ibun   The writings of Nichiren Shōnin.

Goji   *see* Five Periods.

Gosho   *see* Go-ibun.

Great Extent period The third of the Five Periods for classifying sutras by when they were thought to have been taught. This period includes the earlier Mahāyāna sutras such as the *Great Sun Buddha Sutra* and the *Pure Land Sutra*. They are believed to have been taught during the eight years following the Hīnayāna Collection period. *See also* Five Periods.

Great Mandala   The most usual representation of the Most Venerable One. The Great Mandala is a scroll depicting the participants at the Assembly in the Air from the *Lotus Sutra* in the form of the names of the most important representatives in Japanese calligraphy. The participants surround the Odaimoku, Namu Myōhō Renge Kyō, which is written down the middle of the Great Mandala.

Hannya period   *see* Wisdom period.

Higan   Buddhist festivals of about one week that are centered on the spring and autumn equinoxes (approximately March 21st and September 21st). These festivals are times in which to remember one's ancestors and deceased relatives and to dedicate the merit of one's Buddhist practice to all beings, both living and deceased, for their enlightenment.

Hīnayāna   "Lesser Vehicle" in Sanskrit. This term was applied by Mahāyāna Buddhists to the more traditional school of Buddhism when the two schools split a century or so after the Buddha's death. The schools that were so named are today represented by the Theravadan schools of Buddhism, generally found in the more southern areas of Asia. The term is typically used for schools in which the focus is on individual enlightenment instead of on leading all living beings to enlightenment.

Hīnayāna Collection period The second of the Five Periods for classifying sutras by when they were thought to have been taught. This period includes the sutras traditionally ascribed to Theravada Buddhism, and are considered by researchers to be the original scriptures of Buddhism. The version of this canon that was known by T'ien T'ai and by Nichiren Shōnin were actually the Chinese translations of the Theravadan canon in Pali; this translation is known as the Āgama sutras. They are believed to have been taught during the twelve years following the Flower Garland period. *See also* Five Periods.

Hōdō period   *see* Great Extent period.

Hokke-Nehan period *see* Lotus-Nirvana period.

Honmon   *see* Essential Section.

Honzon   *see* Most Venerable One.

Ichinen sanzen   The term for the T'ien T'ai philosophy that every moment of life contains the full breadth of reality, sometimes translated as "three thousand worlds in one moment of thought." Nichiren expanded on this theoretical concept and gave it new application to everyday life. One of the most important things that ichinen sanzen reveals is the potential for Buddhahood within all living beings. This complicated concept is explained in more detail in Chapter 2 of this book.

Ihai   Memorial tablets inscribed with the names of deceased relatives for use on personal and temple altars.

Izu Exile   The second of the four major persecutions that Nichiren Shōnin suffered. He was exiled to the remote and rustic Izu Peninsula on May 12, 1261 for allegedly "disturbing the peace," actually for being critical of the government's support of ineffectual Buddhist schools. This exile lasted for a little less than two years.

Juzu   The "prayer beads" used by many Buddhists. They are often used to count repitions of the Odaimoku. Juzu serve as a symbolic reminder in our daily lives to remain mindful and to attempt to live as the Buddha taught.

Kakochō   A book to record the names and memorial dates of one's ancestors and deceased relatives. Divided by day, these serve as a reminder of when to offer memorial prayers.

Kegon period   *see* Flower Garland period.

Kitō   Though the word "kitō" in Japanese means prayer in a general sense, when we refer specifically to kitō in this book, we are referring to a special kind of ceremony that one will sometimes see performed at some Nichiren Shu temples. These are prayers for attaining Buddhahood in the future and to benefit others by practicing for oneself. They are also prayers to accomplish one's wishes in this lifetime.

Komatsubara Persecution The third of the four major persecutions suffered by Nichiren Shōnin. On November 11, 1264, Nichiren Shōnin was traveling through the Komatsubara woods to a follower's estate when he was ambushed by Kagenobu Tōjō, a local lord that hated Nichiren Shōnin because of his criticism of Tōjō's school of Buddhism. Several disciples were killed in the ambush, and Nichiren Shōnin was injured by a sword stroke that almost killed him but was deflected by his juzu beads.

Latter Age of the Dharma *see* Declining Age of the Dharma.

Lotus-Nirvana period The last and highest of the Five Periods for classifying sutras by when they were thought to have been taught. This period actually includes two sutras, the *Lotus Sutra* itself and the *Nirvana Sutra*. It is believed to have been taught during the final eight years of the Buddha's life following the Wisdom period. *See also* Five Periods.

Lotus Sutra   Fully, the *Wonderful Dharma of the Lotus Flower Sutra* (in Japanese, *Myōhō Renge Kyō*; in Sanskrit, *Saddharma Puṇḍarīka Sutra*). According to Nichiren Shōnin, the ultimate teaching of the Buddha. This scripture is widely revered by many Buddhist schools, and is one of the most cherished works of the Mahāyāna canon.

Mappō   *see* Declining Age of the Dharma.

Māra   "The Tempter" of Buddhist tradition. A symbolic representation of one's inner desires and attachments, Māra personifies the illusions of the world.

Matsubagayatsu Persecution The first of the four major persecutions that Nichiren Shōnin suffered. When he submitted the *Rissho Ankoku Ron* to the government, in which he blamed the suffering of the people on the government's support of ineffectual schools of Buddhism, many supporters of those schools of Buddhism were highly angered and wished to suppress Nichiren Shōnin's views.

On the evening of August 27, 1260, an angry mob of these people attacked his hut, hoping to kill him. Nichiren Shōnin escaped (tradition says he was awoken and led away by a white monkey), but his hut was burned and he had to flee Kamakura.

Mokushō   A wooden clapper that resembles a small drum; used to keep time in Nichiren Shu ceremonies during chanting of sutra passages and the Odaimoku.

Most Venerable One   One of the Three Great Hidden Dharmas. The Most Venerable One is the focus of our devotion and meditative energy. Prescribed by Nichiren Shōnin from his intense study of the Essential Section of the *Lotus Sutra*, it can be represented in several different physical forms. Please see Chapter 2 of this book for a full explanation of the meaning and form of the Most Venerable One.

Mount Gṛdhrakūta   *see* Mount Sacred Eagle.

Mount Sacred Eagle   A hill outside the ancient Indian city of Rājagṛha (about 45 miles southeast of present-day Patna). "Sacred eagle" is the Japanese translation for "vulture." The name in Sanskrit, Gṛdhrakūta, means Mount Vulture. The top of this mount is said to resemble a vulture—however, it is more likely that the name comes from the fact that the city's graveyard was located nearby, so many vultures were seen in the area. Mount Sacred Eagle is the setting of many of the Buddha's later sermons, including the *Lotus Sutra*. In the *Lotus Sutra* itself, Mount Sacred Eagle is often directly named as the place where the events are taking place, or is used to refer to things that happen in our world. Because of this, Nichiren Shōnin often refers to the pure land of the *Lotus Sutra* as Mount Sacred Eagle; of course, the basis of Nichiren Buddhism is that this world is the Buddha's Pure Land. Mount Sacred Eagle as the Pure Land therefore is symbolic to Nichiren Shōnin of the state in which we realize that this world is actually a Buddha land.

Myōhō Renge Kyō   *see* Lotus Sutra.

Namu Myōhō Renge Kyō   *see* Odaimoku.

Obon   *see* Urabon.

Odaimoku   The title of the *Lotus Sutra* and the essence of the Dharma for Nichiren Buddhists. The Odaimoku is Namu Myōhō Renge Kyō. This is the seed that Nichiren planted in the people of the Declining Age of the Dharma so that they can manifest

Buddhahood within themselves. The recitation of the Odaimoku is the essential and central practice of all Nichiren Buddhists, as it serves to nurture the seed of Buddhahood that Nichiren Shōnin planted within us. Its meaning is explained in more detail in Chapter 2 and throughout this book.

Oeshiki   The commemoration of Nichiren Shōnin's death, and the memorial services that surround this observance of October 13, 1282.

Ohigan   *see* Higan.

Pāramitās   *see* Six Perfections.

Precepts   Guidelines for behavior. Mahāyāna Buddhist laypeople generally observe five major precepts, a subset of the precepts that are followed by monks, nuns, and other clergy (Theravadans clergy follow several hundred rules). The five basic Mahāyāna precepts are not to kill, not to steal, not to indulge in harmful sexual behavior, not to lie, and not to become intoxicated. Two things should be remembered: these are not commandments but are perfections to strive for, and these guidelines should be interpreted in the spirit of the Golden Rule.

Precepts Platform   One of the Three Great Hidden Dharmas of Nichiren Buddhism. The term itself refers to the Buddhist tradition of establishing a specific place in which individuals take the Buddhist precepts and are thereby officially recognized as Buddhist clergy or laypeople. In Nichiren Shu, however, the Precepts Platform of the Essential Section of the *Lotus Sutra* is usually understood to be wherever the practitioner recites the Odaimoku.

Provisional Section   The first fourteen chapters of the *Lotus Sutra*. For a complete discussion, see the entry under Essential Section.

Sacred Title   *see* Odaimoku.

Saddharma Puṇḍarīka Sutra   *see* Lotus Sutra.

Sado Exile   The last of the four major persecutions suffered by Nichiren Shōnin was the Tatsunokuchi Persecution. After the government failed to execute him during the Tatsunokuchi Persecution and pardoned him, they still felt that it was necessary to punish Nichiren Shōnin in some way. Therefore, on October 10, 1271, they exiled him to the most remote place possible, Sado Island. With no shelter and no resources, the government assumed that he would die after the first winter, saving them from having to execute him but obtaining the same result. This was not to be, however, and after two and a half years, when Nichiren Shōnin's predictions of a Mongol invasion began to manifest, he was pardoned and allowed to return to the capital. During the Sado Exile, Nichiren Shōnin composed two of his most important essays, *Open Your Eyes to the Lotus Teaching* and *Treatise on Revealing Spiritual Contemplation and the Most Venerable One*. In these essays, he completed his doctrinal teachings based on the *Lotus Sutra*.

Sahā World Our world. "Sahā" means "endurance" in Sanskrit; in the common world, we must endure many kinds of suffering, so this term emphasizes the unsatisfactory nature of the unenlightened world.

Śakyamuni The historical Buddha who attained enlightenment in India in the fifth century B.C.E. This name means "sage of the Śākya clan," and was given to him after his enlightenment since he came from the ruling family of that clan. His given and family name was Siddārtha Gautama.

Sandai hihō *see* Three Great Hidden Dharmas.

Saṅgha The group of people who follows the Buddha's teachings. At one time, saṅgha referred primarily to monks and nuns, but most Mahāyāna schools include laypeople in their definition of saṅgha without reservation.

Shakubuku Japanese for "break and subdue." One of the two methods for propagating the *Lotus Sutra*, it refers to breaking people of their attachments to false doctrines, not to actual physical or verbal violence. Shakubuku is accomplished by direct statements of correct teachings. This is compared to shōju, another way to lead people to the right teaching by moderately encouraging their virtue. Bodhisattva Never Despise in Chapter 20 of the *Lotus Sutra* is an example of the use of shakubuku.

Shakumon *see* Provisional Section.

Shakyō The practice of copying the *Lotus Sutra*, selected phrases from the sutra, or its title (the Odaimoku). Copying the sutra is one of the practices mentioned in the sutra itself as an appropriate way of upholding the sutra.

Shindoku   The Japanese way of pronouncing Chinese writing (the "*on* reading" of Kanji characters). This is the traditional way of reading selections from the *Lotus Sutra*. Sometimes this is referred to as the "Sino-Japanese reading."

Shōdaigyō   A practice in Nichiren Shu which combines intense chanting of the Odaimoku with silent, sitting meditation.

Shōju   One of the two methods for propagating the *Lotus Sutra*. This method is one of "gentle persuasion," usually explained as gently encouraging others to improve themselves others instead of directly telling them the correct teaching. This is compared with shakubuku, the active method of directly leading people to the truth. Chapter 14, "Peaceful Practices," serves as the model for shōju.

Shōmyō   Prayers sung by priests during ceremonies at Nichiren Shu temples. The most common shōmyō are introductory invocations and closing prayers, but some ceremonies include prayers to Buddha, Dharma, and Saṅgha, and other special invocations.

Shōnin   A Japanese title of respect for a learned priest.

Six Perfections   The goals which Mahāyāna Buddhists strive to uphold. Bodhisattvas practice the Six Perfections to lead all living beings to enlightenment. They are giving (or charity), observing the precepts, patience, striving (or energy), meditation, and wisdom.

Tatsunokuchi Persecution   The last of the four major persecutions that Nichiren Shōnin suffered. Because he continued to remonstrate with the government about their ineffectual religious practices, the government arrested Nichiren Shōnin as part of their attempt to round up dissenters as the Mongols threatened the Japanese government. He was sentenced to death by beheading. On September 12, 1271, he was taken to the execution grounds on Tatsunokuchi beach. However, just as the executioner was about to strike, a flash of light appeared in the sky and broke his sword. Frightened by this manifestation, the execution was called off and a messenger was sent to the government to report. However, some of the government ministers who disapproved of beheading a Buddhist priest had already secured a stay of execution; their messenger met the one from the execution ground on the way. Thus, Nichiren Shōnin's life was spared. See the listing under Sado Exile for the rest of the story of the Tatsunokuchi Persecution.

Ten Aspects   The Ten Aspects are a component of ichinen sanzen. They are the aspects that characterize all phenomena, enumerated in the beginning of Chapter 2 of the *Lotus Sutra* at the end of section that is often recited in the daily practice of Nichiren Buddhists. The Ten Aspects are the characteristics of anything regarding its appearance, its nature, its entity, its power, its activity, its primary causes, its environmental causes, its effects, its rewards and retributions, and the unity of the other nine aspects.

Tendai   *see* T'ien T'ai.

Ten Worlds   The Ten Worlds are a general description of the different conditions in which living beings can exist, both from life to life and also, in a symbolic sense, from moment to moment. The Ten Worlds are one of the components that make up ichinen sanzen. They are the worlds of hell, hungry spirits, animals, anger, humans, heaven, śravakas, pratyekabuddhas, bodhisattvas, and Buddhahood. Please see Chapter 2 of this book for a complete description of these worlds.

Theravada   Pali for "the way of the elders." A highly conservative traditional form of Buddhism that relies on the original scriptures in Pali as their canon. They are the remaining school from the traditionalist side of the split that occured within the first several hundred years after the Buddha's death—the schools that were referred to as Hīnayāna by those that came to call themselves Mahāyāna Buddhists.

Three Factors   One of the components of ichinen sanzen, the Three Factors are a way of categorizing the factors that influence the life of any living being. The first is the land in which the being lives, including the physical environment and the society. The second is all the other living beings among which the individual lives. The third is the five aggregates (form, feeling, conception, mind, and perception) which make up the living being him- or herself.

Three Great Hidden Dharmas The defining doctrine of Nichiren Buddhism. The Three Great Hidden Dharmas were discovered by Nichiren Shōnin within the Essential Section of the *Lotus Sutra*. They are the Most Venerable One revealed in the Essential Section, the Precepts Platform prescribed in the Essential Section, and the Odaimoku Chanting founded in the Essential Section. Please see

Chapter 2 of this book for a detailed explanation of the Three Great Hidden Dharmas.

Three Kinds of Action Bodily action, verbal action, and mental action. A Buddhist cannot simply claim belief in the Buddha Dharma; he or she must live the Buddha Dharma by striving to uphold the Buddha's teaching through the Three Kinds of Action: in his or her actions, in his or her words, and with his or her thoughts.

Three Thousand Conditions in One Thought *see* Ichinen Sanzen.

Three Treasures   The three things which all Buddhists take refuge in: the Buddha as the highest teacher, the Buddha's Dharma as the highest teaching, and the Saṅgha as the best community in which to practice those teachings.

T'ien T'ai   The name by which the Chinese Buddhist philosopher Chih-i and the school of Buddhism he founded is commonly known. He lived from 538 to 597 C.E. T'ien T'ai established the supremacy of the *Lotus Sutra* and developed much of the theoretical philosophy of the sutra. However, he did not develop a Buddhist practice that was suitable for laypeople or for the Declining Age of the Dharma.

Urabon   A Buddhist festival to benefit one's ancestors and deceased relatives. This festival usually occurs in mid-July.

Viśiṣṭacāritra   Sanskrit name for Bodhisattva Superb Action.

Wisdom period   The fourth of the Five Periods for classifying sutras by when they were thought to have been taught. This period includes the various sutras that are related to the *Great Perfection of Wisdom Sutra*, also known by its Sanskrit name *Mahāprajñapaāramita Sutra*. It is believed to have been taught during the twenty-two years following the Great Extent period. *See also* Five Periods.

Index

A

B - C

D

E

F - G

H

I - J

O

P - R

W - Z